KATE THOMSEN, M.S., C.A.S.

Parenting Preteens *with a* Purpose

NAVIGATING THE MIDDLE YEARS

SEARCH
INSTITUTE
PRESS

Parenting Preteens with a Purpose:
Navigating the Middle Years

Kate Thomsen, M.S., C.A.S.

The following are registered trademarks
of Search Institute: Search Institute®
and Developmental Assets®.

Search Institute Press
Copyright © 2008 by Search Institute

All rights reserved. No parts of this
publication may be reproduced in any
manner, mechanical or electronic, without prior permission from the publisher
except in brief quotations or summaries
in articles or reviews, or as individual
activity sheets for educational use only.
For additional permission, write to
Permissions at Search Institute.

At the time of publication, all facts and
figures cited herein are the most current available; all telephone numbers,
addresses, and Web site URLs are
accurate and active; all publications,
organizations, Web sites, and other
resources exist as described in this
book; and all efforts have been made
to verify them. The author and Search
Institute make no warranty or guar-
antee concerning the information and
materials given out by organizations
or content found at Web sites that are
cited herein, and we are not responsible
for any changes that occur after this
book's publication. If you find an error
or believe that a resource listed herein is
not as described, please contact Client
Services at Search Institute.

10 9 8 7 6 5 4 3 2 1
Printed on acid-free paper in the United
States of America.

Search Institute
615 First Avenue Northeast, Suite 125
Minneapolis, MN 55413
www.search-institute.org
612-376-8955 • 800-888-7828

ISBN-13: 978-1-57482-199-4

Credits
Editors: Susan Wootten, Ruth Taswell
Book Design: Jeenee Lee

Library of Congress
Cataloging-in-Publication Data

Thomsen, Kate.
  Parenting preteens with a purpose :
navigating the middle years / by Kate
Thomsen.
    p. cm.
  Includes bibliographical references
and index.
  ISBN-13: 978-1-57482-199-4
  (pbk. : alk. paper)
  ISBN-10: 1-57482-199-7
  (pbk. : alk. paper)
  1. Preteens. 2. Parenting.
  3. Adolescent psychology.
  4. Communication in the family.
  I. Title.
HQ777.15.T56 2008
649'.124--dc22

                        2007043876

Dedicated with gratitude to my parents, Grace and John Reilly,

and to my parents-in-law, Jo and Bob Thomsen.

You gave us what we needed to turn possibilities into realities.

CONTENTS

ACKNOWLEDGMENTS

I gratefully acknowledge Search Institute's former Director of Publishing, Claudia Hoffacker, who accepted and shepherded my proposal for a book for parents. I appreciate having an opportunity to make this contribution. I would like to give a very special thanks to Susan Wootten for being so encouraging and helpful to me as I worked my way through this manuscript. You have made this experience exciting, rewarding, and relatively stress-free.

I would like to thank my mother and father, Grace and John Reilly, for working so hard to nurture, educate, and instill solid values in all seven of their children. I would also like to thank my mother and father-in-law, Jo and Bob Thomsen, for raising their son to be a great husband and parenting partner with integrity, generosity, character, and kindness. I am eternally grateful to my two sons, Dan and Patrick, for being patient with me as I felt my way through their early years and adolescence. Sorry, Dan, for using you as the guinea pig, but I had to start somewhere! Thank you both for forgiving my mistakes. Without you two, this book would have been impossible to write.

Thank you to my six older siblings, Regina, Rosemary, Carol, Peggy, John, and Mary, who offered me their parenting expertise when I was a preteen—even when I didn't ask for it! I appreciate now that you were offering support and boundaries, and I thank you for those assets.

I would also like to thank members of the Chittenango Central School District's Parent Teacher Association for agreeing to try out some of the tips offered in this book. Your feedback was instrumental in helping me forge ahead with this project. Thank you for attending my lectures and for working so hard at being the best parents you can be.

And finally, thank you to all the parents I have ever leaned on when I needed support. Your words of wisdom and kind understanding have been priceless.

INTRODUCTION

Remember the popular '70s song, "Stuck in the
Middle with You"? It was one of my favorites. During
my kids' middle school years, I often found myself
humming it when I was stuck for answers on how to
deal with the many issues facing them.

The preteen years can be filled with joy and wonder, but sometimes you may find yourself heading in
directions you hadn't anticipated. While you'll often
come up with satisfying solutions to parenting challenges
on your own, at times those solutions may not be quite
so obvious.

My kids, like many preteens, wondered whether
they were popular enough, athletic enough, too tall or
too short, too chubby or too thin. And they had other
concerns: Why is my face breaking out? What are other
kids instant-messaging about me? Is it okay to be smart?
Can I admit that I like someone? Why does my mother
buy me such geeky clothes?

Neither song lyrics nor my own youthful experiences completely prepared me for the task of parenting
my preteens. Many of the issues that 8- to 12-year-old
children face today are different from the ones I faced as
a kid. I had no cell phone, computer with Internet access,
or TV in my bedroom. While today's preteens confront
the same developmental issues of 8- to 12-year-olds in
past decades, they also face new ones unique to the high-
tech age.

The term "gear up" appropriately suggests the task ahead of you—preparing yourself with effective tools and strategies to guide your children through the next phase of their development. So gear up and (as the Boy Scouts and Girl Scouts say) be prepared! It is far better to anticipate preteen parenting issues and plan possible responses to them than to be caught off guard without strategies at the ready.

With a little advance preparation, you'll feel more confident and less "stuck in the middle" when your preteen child poses a new challenge to you. The preteen years truly can be exciting and fun, especially if you feel comfortable with your parenting skills and can relax and enjoy your children as they begin to transform themselves into young adults.

WHO IS THIS BOOK FOR?

Every person who helps raise a preteen child will find this book valuable. The term "parent" is used here to describe an adult who guides, loves, and is invested positively in the life of a child.

Today, families include traditional two-parent households, as well as those headed by divorced, widowed, and never-married parents; gay and lesbian parents; adoptive parents; grandparents-as parents; long-distance parents; and foster parents. And many teachers, clergy, counselors, therapists, and other adults who may not have kids of their own also lovingly parent many kids over the course of their careers. This book is for all of you who care enough to make the time to parent the young people in your lives.

BUILDING ASSETS FOR YOUR PRETEEN

Gearing up to parent children in their preteen years starts with your attitude and perspective on parenting. While it would be nice to have a silver bullet that solves all dilemmas and reveals all parenting answers, of course no such solution exists. But having parented two preteens into adulthood, I'd like to share with you an image that can help you keep a positive perspective.

Did you ever toss pebbles into a pool of water when you were a kid? The ripples that flowed outward in every direction come to mind when the subject turns to parenting preteens and raising competent, healthy kids. When you interact in positive, respectful ways with your children, your actions are like so many pebbles tossed into puddles, and the rippling effects of your actions are much greater than the actions themselves.

Parenting choices you make every day may sometimes seem mundane or routine, but simple actions can build important Developmental Assets for kids. When you deliberately provide assets—relationships, structure, opportunities, and guidance—for your kids, you help them grow into healthy, happy, and successful young adults. Establishing routines for homework, chores, and family dinner, as well as participating together in a faith community or holding weekend family nights, may not seem like earth-shattering practices, but the effects of these routines on preteen children can be amazing. It's like throwing pebbles into a puddle—the more ripples you produce, the better off your children are.

WHAT ARE DEVELOPMENTAL ASSETS?

Search Institute, a Minnesota-based education research organization, has identified 40 Developmental Assets that young people need to grow into healthy, successful, competent adults. The Developmental Assets represent a positive, research-based framework for youth development and offer concrete direction to adults parenting children from birth to adulthood. Search Institute divides the 40 Developmental Assets into the eight general categories of Support, Empowerment, Boundaries and Expectations, Constructive Use of Time, Commitment to Learning, Positive Values, Social Competencies, and Positive Identity.

Over time, Search Institute has continued to learn about the 40 assets from the survey responses of more than one million 6th through 12th graders across the United States and abroad, through direct observation, and as a result of research done by experts in the field of positive youth development. In addition, researchers have conducted extensive literature reviews of more than 1,200 scientific studies.

Search Institute's research has shown that young people who report high numbers of Developmental Assets are better able to resist risk-taking behaviors, perform better academically, and handle life's challenges more resiliently. In general, children who report more assets experience better outcomes in life.

The 40 Developmental Assets for Middle Childhood (ages 8–12)

Support

1. *Family support*—Family life provides high levels of love and support.
2. *Positive family communication*—Parent(s) and child communicate positively. Child feels comfortable seeking advice and counsel from parent(s).
3. *Other adult relationships*—Child receives support from adults other than her or his parent(s).
4. *Caring neighborhood*—Child experiences caring neighbors.
5. *Caring school climate*—Relationships with teachers and peers provide a caring, encouraging school environment.
6. *Parent involvement in schooling*—Parent(s) are actively involved in helping the child succeed in school.

Empowerment

7. *Community values children*—Child feels valued and appreciated by adults in the community.
8. *Children as resources*—Child is included in decisions at home and in the community.
9. *Service to others*—Child has opportunities to help others in the community.
10. *Safety*—Child feels safe at home, at school, and in her or his neighborhood.

Boundaries and Expectations

11. *Family boundaries*—Family has clear and consistent rules and consequences and monitors the child's whereabouts.
12. *School boundaries*—School provides clear rules and consequences.
13. *Neighborhood boundaries*—Neighbors take responsibility for monitoring the child's behavior.

14. *Adult role models*—Parent(s) and other adults in the child's family, as well as nonfamily adults, model positive, responsible behavior.
15. *Positive peer influence*—Child's closest friends model positive, responsible behavior.
16. *High expectations*—Parent(s) and teachers expect the child to do her or his best at school and in other activities.

Constructive Use of Time
17. *Creative activities*—Child participates in music, art, drama, or creative writing two or more times per week.
18. *Child programs*—Child participates two or more times per week in co-curricular school activities or structured community programs for children.
19. *Religious community*—Child attends religious programs or services one or more times per week.
20. *Time at home*—Child spends some time most days both in high-quality interaction with parents and doing things at home other than watching TV or playing video games.

INTERNAL ASSETS

Commitment to Learning
21. *Achievement motivation*—Child is motivated and strives to do well in school.
22. *Learning engagement*—Child is responsive, attentive, and actively engaged in learning at school and enjoys participating in learning activities outside of school.
23. *Homework*—Child usually hands in homework on time.
24. *Bonding to adults at school*—Child cares about teachers and other adults at school.
25. *Reading for pleasure*—Child enjoys and engages in reading for fun most days of the week.

Positive Values
26. *Caring*—Parent(s) tell the child it is important to help other people.
27. *Equality and social justice*—Parent(s) tell the child it is important to speak up for equal rights for all people.

28. *Integrity*—Parent(s) tell the child it is important to stand up for one's beliefs.
29. *Honesty*—Parent(s) tell the child it is important to tell the truth.
30. *Responsibility*—Parent(s) tell the child it is important to accept personal responsibility for behavior.
31. *Healthy lifestyle*—Parent(s) tell the child it is important to have good health habits and an understanding of healthy sexuality.

Social Competencies

32. *Planning and decision making*—Child thinks about decisions and is usually happy with results of her or his decisions.
33. *Interpersonal competence*—Child cares about and is affected by other people's feelings, enjoys making friends, and, when frustrated or angry, tries to calm her- or himself.
34. *Cultural competence*—Child knows and is comfortable with people of different racial, ethnic, and cultural backgrounds and with her or his own cultural identity.
35. *Resistance skills*—Child can stay away from people who are likely to get her or him in trouble and is able to say no to doing wrong or dangerous things.
36. *Peaceful conflict resolution*—Child attempts to resolve conflict nonviolently.

Positive Identity

37. *Personal power*—Child feels he or she has some influence over things that happen in her or his life.
38. *Self-esteem*—Child likes and is proud to be the person he or she is.
39. *Sense of purpose*—Child sometimes thinks about what life means and whether there is a purpose for her or his life.
40. *Positive view of personal future*—Child is optimistic about her or his personal future.

HOW DID YOU GET *YOUR* ASSETS?

You may remember a particular person or experience from childhood or adolescence that made a huge difference in your life. Possibly a teacher or neighbor asked for your help and made you feel valued. Perhaps an experience in school, at summer camp, or in a part-time job helped you discover how well you could do something. Or maybe your parents consistently encouraged you to do well in school, and so you did. In retrospect, you may see how such experiences helped you become the person you are today. Even if you didn't have a positive childhood, you may remember someone who mentored you and threw pebbles into your puddle.

You can nurture Developmental Assets in your own preteens by providing opportunities that will give them support and the necessary skills to grow into competent, healthy, contributing members of society. Everyone has the power to be an asset builder for kids. This book can help you understand and apply the Developmental Asset framework as an essential tool in your parenting.

Take a moment to reflect on how you developed your strengths. If you can recognize who and what contributed to your personal growth, you can accelerate the positive development of your kids and other kids with whom you interact. And once you familiarize yourself with the asset framework, you can also be intentional about the parenting actions you engage in. Your preteen will benefit from developing as many assets as you and other adults are able to support.

WHAT DO ASSETS DO?

Assets enable people of all ages to rise above adversity. Educational researchers report three important foundations in resilient people who seem to handle life's challenges well:

- They have benefited from a long-term, supportive relationship with at least one caring adult (a parent or surrogate parent, such as a grandparent, neighbor, or teacher).

- They have had opportunities to contribute in meaningful ways to their family or community.

- Other people have set high expectations for them, and given them appropriate support (Benard, 1991).

Developmental Assets relate to each of these three areas. Building assets for children ensures that they are more likely to be resilient, able to handle life's challenges, and develop into competent adults.

THE DEVELOPMENTAL ASSETS FRAMEWORK PROVIDES SUPPORT AND DIRECTION

Parenting can be a lonely job. You might second-guess yourself, especially when you compare yourself to other parents, or your kids push you to be like other parents. Perhaps you've heard, "Why am I the only one who isn't allowed to see this movie?" Such questions may throw you into conflict over your rules. It's often easier to say yes to children than to stand firm against whining and accusations.

Children need to have as many assets as possible to successfully navigate their way into adulthood. While it's ideal for a child to have 30 to 40 assets, on average young people report just 18.6 assets (in responses from almost 150,000 6th through 12th graders, who participated in nationwide *Search Institute Profiles of Student Life: Attitudes and Behaviors* surveys through 2003). Realize that asset building is a life-long process. Although the challenges to raising children who have values and character may seem formidable, you can do it!

Assets provide a protective influence that helps kids resist the pressure to participate in risk-taking behaviors. The more assets your child has, the better your child's academic achievement will be and the better the choices your child will make regarding illegal substance use and early sexual activity. The influences of television, music, movies, video games, computer technology, advertising, and peer pressure (which both kids and parents feel) sometimes make your parenting job seem daunting. But parenting with a positive asset framework can give you the support, encouragement, skills, and belief in your own convictions to successfully guide your children into productive adulthood.

LOOK FOR ASSET-BUILDING IDEAS

Use this book as a parenting companion, teaching tool, and discussion stimulator. You'll find numerous tips and suggestions, along with text and online references for further reading.

- *Part One—Becoming an Asset-Building Parent* defines Developmental Assets and asset categories, and applies them to preteen parenting tips and strategies. You'll also find a review of the emotional, intellectual, and physical capabilities of 8- to 12-year-old children. Part One includes valuable *Reflection and Discussion* inventories that can help you gain insights into your own parenting behaviors.

- *Part Two—Taking Care of Yourself* offers practical suggestions for taking care of yourself during a time of change, growth, and adjustment for both you and your preteen. Strong, healthy, relaxed parents help to nurture strong, healthy, relaxed children.

- *Part Three—Taking Care of Your Preteen* addresses specific issues in alphabetical order that parents sometimes struggle with and offers insights and strategies to help deal effectively with those issues when they arise. You'll find a connection between each topic and the relevant Developmental Assets it touches upon.

As you use this book, consider forming a discussion group with other parents, and join forces to build assets together in your kids. Your discussion group might decide to focus on one asset category at a time and take action to build those assets over a two-week period. When you get back together as a group, share what worked well and what didn't. Coach one another. Cheer each other on. And remember, there is support and safety in numbers!

TAKE HEART AND TRUST YOUR WISDOM

Parenting is a journey without a roadmap. Even parents with the purest intentions run into obstacles. The best navigational system is your own intuition. When you know something doesn't feel right, have faith in yourself. When you sense that your child is struggling, trust your instincts.

Deal directly with problems, and don't hesitate to seek help from doctors, counselors, school personnel, and other experts. Intervening early when issues first arise often allows you to avoid bigger problems later. Use this book as a resource, and use other parents as sources of support. Help is out there—you don't have to struggle with the preteen years alone. And offer your support to other parents.

Enjoy your job as a parent of a preteen. Before you know it, that job will be done and you'll move on to different challenges. With the help of this book, may you find the excitement and joy inherent in parenting preteens.

IDENTITY BOUNDARIES

part one:

Becoming an Asset-Building Parent

VALUES EMPOWERMENT

PARENTING WITH THE DEVELOPMENTAL ASSETS FRAMEWORK

You know the only people who are always sure about the proper way to raise children? Those who've never had any. BILL COSBY, *FATHERHOOD*

There may be no more important job in the world than that of parenting. It is serious and important, rewarding and full of joyful possibilities. I'm sure I learned more from my parenting job than from any other job I've held, before or since. But while learning more than ever, I sometimes found myself looking for answers. Many parents feel this way at one time or another— it comes with the territory. The good news is there is on-the-job training.

IT TAKES ONE TO KNOW ONE

When I had my own kids, I finally understood my parents. I began to understand their guidelines and values, pride in my accomplishments, worries, admonitions, sacrifices, strengths, and wisdom. I acknowledged what they did well, and thought about what they might have done differently. I realized with a bit of trepidation that it was my turn to try to do as well or even better for my own kids.

Children develop assets as a consequence of the actions of the adults with whom they live. Assets cannot develop without the deliberate efforts of parents, caring adults, and communities that offer youth guidance, opportunities, and relationships. The responsibility for growing assets for your children is yours.

Spotlight on Developmental Assets

Search Institute groups the 40 Developmental Assets into eight asset categories as follows:

External Assets
Support
Empowerment
Boundaries and Expectations
Constructive Use of Time

Internal Assets
Commitment to Learning
Positive Values
Social Competencies
Positive Identity

External assets are the Developmental Assets categories that relate directly to support, opportunities, expectations, limits, and activities that are available to young people within the family, school, and community. Adults can help develop external assets in youth through relationships focused on intentional actions and positive role modeling.

Internal assets relate directly to young people's attitudes, values, competencies, and personal identity. Adults can help preteens develop internal assets by providing nurturing opportunities and excellent role modeling.

While it's true that children enter this world equipped with unique genetic gifts and challenges, their experiences as infants, children, preteens, and teens also profoundly impact their brain chemistry and mold their brains' responses. For example, social skills, language, empathy, decision making, impulse control, and motivation to achieve are all hard-wired into the brain through a child's direct experience. As a parent, you provide the opportunities and experiences for your children, and monitor the experiences they choose for themselves. It helps to be familiar with children's developmental stages to do this well.

NOTHING STAYS THE SAME FOREVER

A parent's job changes as a child develops. Do you remember walking behind your toddler, bent with arms outstretched, ready to catch her when she stumbled? Now you find yourself walking beside your preteen, guiding her into adulthood. You still want to protect and teach her, but it's helpful to change your mode of delivery to accommodate your child's growth and progress.

This section presents important information about preteen development, including recent research findings on the adolescent brain. With this information, you can better judge how closely you need to guide preteens and when it is appropriate to let them discover their own way. These nuggets may give you insights into behavior that previously puzzled you. New brain-imaging technology helps shed light on many previously puzzling aspects of adolescent behavior, including key differences in the brain development of boys and girls.

SEE YOUR KIDS AS INDIVIDUALS

The exciting, wonderful, and often confusing thing about the preteen years is that it's difficult to define this age by physical, emotional, or cognitive characteristics. If you observed a large group of 8- to 12-year-olds for a period of time, you'd see some surge ahead of their grade academically, while others lagged behind. Some would start to develop physically mature bodies; others would be months or years away from that. Some would manage their emotions fairly well; others would dissolve into tears when frustrated. Some would be socially ahead of

Why Do Girls Talk More Than Boys?

Family therapist and author Michael Gurian notes that girls' brains are characterized by stronger neural connections in the temporal lobes, which leads to more detailed, sensory-related memory storage, better listening skills, and better discrimination among various tones of voice. This leads, among other things, to greater verbal ability and more detail in girls' writing assignments.

Boys' brains occupy half the space used by girls for verbal-emotive functioning. Their brains produce less serotonin (a neurotransmitter) and less oxytocin (the human bonding hormone), making boys less likely to want to sit still and talk empathetically with a friend. Boys would rather move objects through the air. If you want preteen boys to talk to you, bounce a ball with them or take them on a hike while you talk (Gurian and Stevens, 2004).

their years; others would be less adept. Some would be organized and focused in school; others would be forgetful and scattered. It's good to remember that each child has his or her own style and inner clock for development.

Theories and information can help to guide your actions and examine your expectations for your children. But use such information wisely and cautiously, because there will always be exceptions to the rules. Some boys chatter away. Some girls like to throw footballs. Stages of development are general; it is when a child is far outside the norm that there is cause for concern. Many kids who seem "out of sync" are able to catch up as their brains physically mature.

Remember, too, that experience molds the brain. Positive experiences lead to better learning. For example, if a boy is slow to read and write, the culprit may be a lack of maturity or experience rather than a learning disability. The act of reading with comprehension is complicated and involves the ability to integrate physical coordination, past experience, memory, and attention. Children will have more positive school experiences with reading and writing tasks when they also have had many opportunities to be read to and interact with adults who speak clearly, using standard grammar and interesting vocabulary.

Of course, in some cases young people will need professional intervention if they are not progressing at the rate of most other students their age. When a child lags far behind his or her peers, make inquiries of teachers, physicians, and other professionals. Pediatricians and school professionals can offer useful guidelines for determining whether intervention is needed. If a child is frustrated or discouraged because he or she is not doing well academically in spite of good effort, then assistance is necessary before the child internalizes the belief "I can't."

SUPPORT

Search Institute research confirms that children benefit most when they receive support from adults in their home, school, and neighborhood. The six Support assets include those connected with you and your home, as well as those focusing on supportive relationships with other caring adults.

Support Means Relationships

When it comes to teaching preteens how to build relationships, parents, caregivers, and other adults lead the way. Children learn from what adults do and say, but also from what adults don't do and say. Preteens care what adults think, and watch what they do. In fact, when kids refuse to use illegal drugs, the reason they most often cite is that they know their parents would disap-

Erikson's Theory of Identity Development

In 1950, developmental psychologist Erik Erikson proposed a theory of psychosocial development in his classic work *Childhood and Society* that describes eight stages through which a person moves over a lifetime. If an individual successfully deals with and resolves the challenges inherent in each stage of identity formation, he moves on to the next stage. Erikson argued that unresolved problems within one stage are bound to be repeated in future stages.

The challenge all children must resolve in middle childhood, Erikson maintained, is that of industry vs. inferiority. The main question children this age grapple with is "Am I successful at what I do, or am I worthless?" If adults support preteens' efforts, they develop a sense of competence. A child who is not supported may develop feelings of inferiority. Since the child's central task in middle childhood is managing school and education tasks, school success is crucial to this stage of development (Erikson, 1963).

prove. Parents have enormous power, if they choose to use it (see "Online Resources" on page 173).

Build relationships early with your kids. Don't wait for a "right" time. It's easier to build solid relationships when children are young, because they are more naturally open to your attempts to connect. To their way of thinking, parents know everything, and parental attention means they matter. Later, when peers begin to assume a more prominent role in preteens' lives, you will more likely have established a solid base of mutual respect, love, and trust with your preteen. Having a preteen who willingly confides in you can help make the preteen years enjoyable and exciting.

The Support asset category places relationships at

its core. A summary by Search Institute researchers of aggregated data results from national *Search Institute Profiles of Student Life: Attitudes and Behaviors* surveys reveals that most youth surveyed (68 percent) report having family support, but less than one third (28 percent) report having positive family communication. Parents need to work intentionally on building support assets, since so many other assets hinge upon this group (Search Institute, 2005).

Building Positive Family Communication

Many parents may wait too long to get to know their kids; some never have the really important talks. I'm talking about all kinds of talks—about favorite TV shows, the funny things that happen at school, why some kids are mean, whose eyes they inherited, and why animals and older people need our kindness. Establishing good communication with preteens—and really listening to them—should start long before problems necessitate tough conversations.

Between school, after-school activities, social lives, homework, sports commitments, television, video games, computer use, and parents' own work and social commitments, parents and preteens often live parallel, rather than intersecting, lives. Some families sit at a table to eat a meal together only a few times a year. This makes it difficult to build intimate family relationships. It is important to keep in mind that it's never too late to begin building a relationship with your child, but it is best to start early. Parents must make regular "deposits" in their parent-child relationship "accounts" long before they need to make "withdrawals."

The Family: A Preteen's Most Important Influence

"Studies have shown that while peer influence and emotional closeness to peers increase during early adolescence, peer relationships supplement but do not replace ties with parents. Although adolescents report they look to their peer groups for companionship and for guidance in some aspects of behavior, such as dress, music, hairstyle, and entertainment, they look to their families for affection, identification, social and moral values, and help in solving big problems or making important decisions" (Center for Early Adolescence, 1992).

Connect with Your Preteen *Now*

Establishing good communication with your preteen is the first step in making sure your relationship with your preteen is solid. Try both new and tried-and-true activities together. Share family rituals. Simply spend time (not money) together.

You can help your preteen develop good decision-making skills, too. Talk about positive and negative choices you both observe and hear about in school, at home, at work, and in the community. Talk about both great and tough experiences your child has with friends, at school, in sports, and in other areas. If possible, offer a positive interpretation your preteen can take away from the experience.

In the absence of positive family and community relationships, preteens may find negative peer groups that make them feel connected and appreciated. It is difficult for parents to intervene in destructive peer relations unless the parent-child relationship is already established.

❗ *Parenting Tips: Building Positive Family Communication*

Tip 1. Treat your kids as well as you treat your friends.

To build a solid relationship with your preteen, no matter his or her age, think about the people you like to spend time with. Are they fun? Do they make you laugh? Do they listen to you and ask questions that let you know they're interested in what you're doing? Do they hold values similar to yours, respect your differences, and keep their commitments? If so, you'll understand what preteens are also looking for in their family relationships. When you can answer your preteen's questions honestly and willingly, and share their experiences, hopes, and dreams, you will have made a solid effort toward establishing a lasting relationship. If you treat your child as well as you treat your adult friends, he or she will want to spend time with you as well.

Tip 2. Make time and spend time.

Don't be discouraged if your preteen rejects your first attempts at spending time together. It may seem odd to a child to have a parent initiate conversations or suggest joint activities when that previously has not been the case. Your preteen may wonder if you have a hidden agenda, or what he or she has done to deserve the sudden attention! Keep trying.

Reflection and Discussion:
Family Support

ASSET 1: Family Support
ASSET 2: Positive Family
Communication

Take a look at the following statements to see how you're doing in the relationship-building area. Think about your responses and look for ways you can take positive steps toward a sound relationship with your preteen.

```
. · ALWAYS
   · · SOMETIMES
      · · NEVER
```

☐ ☐ ☐ I spend unstructured time with my preteen, doing what he or she likes to do.

☐ ☐ ☐ I don't let TV, video games, or computer use distract us from having a conversation.

☐ ☐ ☐ I put aside cleaning, work, or socializing so I can spend time with my child.

☐ ☐ ☐ I ask for a rain check and make a future date when my preteen and I must cancel or postpone an activity we had planned to do.

☐ ☐ ☐ I believe my kids when they say "no problem" if I must cancel our plans (and I look for signs that might say otherwise).

☐ ☐ ☐ I enjoy my preteen. We can get silly and laugh together.

☐ ☐ ☐ I sometimes ask what my preteen would like to do, and then do it without grumbling or checking my watch.

☐ ☐ ☐ I attend my preteen's games or performances whenever I can.

☐ ☐ ☐ When I am upset with my preteen's actions, I ask myself "Under what circumstances would I have done the same thing?"

☐ ☐ ☐ I refrain from criticizing my preteen's selection of music or other choices until we have a chance to discuss them.

☐ ☐ ☐ I find ways to support my child's academic progress.

Reflection and Discussion:
Caring Adult Support

Think about the following statements and see how you're doing in helping your preteen develop positive relationships with other adults. As you think about your responses, you may see ways you can take actions that lead to positive adult relationships for your preteen.

· · ALWAYS
· · · SOMETIMES
· · · NEVER

☐ ☐ ☐ I contribute to a caring school climate for my preteen and his or her peers.

☐ ☐ ☐ I take time to contact my preteen's teacher to offer him or her assistance or to express concerns.

☐ ☐ ☐ I greet other kids in my neighborhood by name.

☐ ☐ ☐ I offer our house as a place where kids are welcome to visit and hang out.

☐ ☐ ☐ I keep snacks on hand to make kids feel welcome.

☐ ☐ ☐ I interact with my kids' friends and show genuine interest in them.

☐ ☐ ☐ I introduce my children to my adult friends.

☐ ☐ ☐ I teach and model for my children appropriate ways to meet adults (make eye contact, hold out the right hand for a handshake, say "It's nice to meet you").

☐ ☐ ☐ I encourage my preteens to assist elderly people in our neighborhood without expecting anything in return.

☐ ☐ ☐ Our family socializes with other neighborhood families.

☐ ☐ ☐ Our family encourages reading and "electronics-free" study time.

- *Offer alternate times for future activities.*

- *Invite your child to choose the activity.*

- *Explain that you realize you were missing out on being with your preteen and are hoping to do better.*

- *Be honest and genuine.* Kids can tell when you are being real and when you are not.

Tip 3. Use car time.

There is nothing like being a captive audience in a car, facing forward with seatbelt firmly in place. Eye contact is optional, and no one can leave! Parents can hold great conversations while riding in cars with their kids, especially with preteens who sometimes are unsure of themselves. It is important for them to be able to "save face" when they talk about difficult issues. Use car time wisely to say the things you want your child to hear or to ask questions. Don't be surprised if one answer leads to more questions.

Volunteer to take your preteens and their friends places, and make a point of introducing yourself to their parents. Use car time to get to know your preteens' friends, too. Kids often forget that the driver can hear everything that's being said. It's a great opportunity to get a glimpse of what's going on in kids' lives: whom the popular (and unpopular) teachers are, the truth about bullies, and plans yet to be discussed and approved. It's well worth taking the long way home.

Tip 4. Quality time can be simple.

How about watching (and discussing) some of the Saturday morning cartoons that preteens like to watch while sipping hot cocoa together and nestling under warm blankets on the couch? It may help you understand why certain shows appeal to preteens and offer insight into their sense of humor. (Be careful not to judge their choices harshly in order to keep the lines of communication open.) Ride bikes or take walks with your preteen to no place special, or toss a ball outside together. Play board games. Watch a movie. The activity doesn't have to be a big event. It is the time spent together that is important.

Tip 5. Make it fun and practical.
Parents and kids often split up at the mall, only to meet back later and rush off to the next activity—not exactly asset-building time. With a little creativity, parents can make shopping (or other activities) together a productive, relationship-building experience.

Focus on teaching your preteens how to shop and spend money responsibly. Encourage them to observe how you shop, learn store etiquette, and listen to the reasoning behind your purchases. Older preteens can begin to shop on their own, and report back to you what they bought and why they believe they made good choices. All this takes is a little preparation before the shopping event, and a little reflective processing afterward. If you have more than one preteen, make time to occasionally shop with each one alone to spend some one-on-one time together.

Remember, learning occurs in the processing of events. Talking about what happened, why it happened, and what you might do similarly or differently next time makes all the difference. And your parent-child relationship will continue to build.

Tip 6. Give kids some say.
Preteens need to know that they are more important to you than any activity you share together. If you want to plan and share activities as a family, then offer them some say in those activities. Ask what they would like to

do, and then join in cheerfully, without judgment. The important thing is that you spend time with them.

You probably make occasional compromises when you plan activities with your friends, so why not do the same for your kids? Compromise will come more readily for them if you model it first. It might sound something like, "Last week we saw the movie I wanted to see. So this week why don't we choose something you want to do?"

Tip 7. Change the script.

If you tire of hearing the same answers to the questions you ask your preteen, how about changing the questions? Or, better yet, don't ask questions at all. Putting your words into a statement can be far more effective.

If it is difficult to get your preteen to talk, why not start by talking about yourself? Instead of the same old pattern, talk about how your day went, and you may get a response unlike any of the scripted answers you're accustomed to hearing:

Parent: "What a frustrating day!"

Preteen: "Yeah? What happened?"

Parent: "My phone rang nonstop, people kept interrupting me, and I couldn't get any work done. I had to bring it all home to do tonight after dinner."

Preteen: "That's too bad. Looks like we're both stuck with homework tonight."

Parent: "You're right. At least now we can do it together."

When parents change their tune, a meaningful conversation can take place that may likely increase understanding on both sides. Children can feel good that their parents are willing to share some of their feelings and frustrations—and feel validated to be treated more like adults. Parents can empathize with their preteens and feel good about engaging in meaningful conversation with them.

Tip 8. Take a chance!

When my son was in the eighth grade, I suggested to some of his friends' parents that we have a family picnic. Although we were acquainted, we weren't close friends. I felt somewhat shy about approaching the other parents, but am glad now that I took the chance. We held the picnic, and all the families came. The boys loved it, and so did the parents. The kids seemed to like the fact that their parents enjoyed each other's company as much as the boys enjoyed being together.

In future years, we got together at least once a year, and still continue to gather, even though our sons have grown into adulthood. We look forward to our sons' visits home and enjoy hearing about their accomplishments. So take a chance on extending hospitality to parents you may not know well—you may find friendships grow where you least expect them, and you will appreciate the support and encouragement such contacts can provide.

EMPOWERMENT

One of a preteen's developmental tasks is to cultivate abilities that allow her or him to become a confident, successful individual. Preteens need to see themselves as worthwhile and capable. If not, they may develop feelings of helplessness or inadequacy and become "stuck." They may not want to take risks in their learning, or may even stop trying. Some may also act disruptively in school to distract others from seeing that they are struggling with schoolwork.

You can help preteens develop their many abilities if you focus on making sure they feel safe physically and emotionally, at home and at school. When kids feel safe, they're more likely to take the risks that naturally arise during the preteen years and that are critical to their healthy development.

Spotlight on the Empowerment Assets

Four Developmental Assets make up the category of
Empowerment. These assets are:

7. Community values children
8. Children as resources
9. Service to others
10. Safety

Preteens *Do* Make Mistakes

Have you ever noticed that babies are not afraid to fail
as they learn the critical skills of talking, walking, and
manipulating objects? It's when kids experience harsh or
overly critical responses to their mistakes from people
who matter to them—parents, peers, siblings, other
adults, or, for some anxious kids, themselves—that they
learn to fear failure.

Imagine what life would be like if babies were
afraid to learn to walk or talk because they didn't want
to make a mistake. You'd be pushing a stroller forever!
But understanding parents *expect* their babies to take
time to learn to walk, and therefore have lots of patience
with them.

Preteens also need lots of opportunities to try and
to fail without concern for their skill level. Encourage
your child to try a new sport without worrying whether
she's a star athlete. Tell him that you'd rather he tried a
challenging school project that interests him rather than
sticking to a topic he already knows well and has lost
interest in. Give your preteen the opportunity to invite
friends over without making all the arrangements yourself. Becoming an empowered preteen is about trying new
things and learning from each attempt.

Kids this age also need to know it's okay to ask lots

of questions, seek help, and voice their hopes and fears. So cheer their efforts, and redirect their mistakes. In fact, expect mistakes, and soothe their egos when necessary.

As preteens learn and practice their new social and academic skills, they may no longer seem as sweet and innocent as they were earlier. They are beginning to develop adult physical characteristics, but it will be some time before they become as mature as they look. During these important transitional childhood years, you can do lots of things to help your preteen feel empowered. The first thing? Make mistakes "safe" for them to make.

Why Make Mistakes Safe to Make?

Kids cooperate, learn, and meet your expectations when they feel safe and respected. Kids who are willing to take risks and learn from their experiences will develop competence and self-esteem. Research indicates that many resilient people have high expectations placed on them, and, as a result, do better in life. An important caveat is that high expectations are effective asset builders only when set at appropriate levels, and when appropriate support is available to assist the preteen in achieving them.

Placing high expectations on young people can be damaging if the necessary foundational skills are lacking. Expecting too much, too soon, can be frustrating for a preteen and may cause that child to shut down and stop trying. Too much criticism of a child who is already doing his or her best is a sure way to thwart a child's growth. On the other hand, expecting too little from kids is harmful, too. Kids may interpret low expectations to mean they are not competent enough to be expected to contribute.

Educators emphasize that for students to learn well, they must feel the correct amount of stress or level of concern, which refers to how a child perceives the

Reflection and Discussion: Empowerment

ASSET 7: Community Values Children
ASSET 8: Children as Resources
ASSET 9: Service to Others
ASSET 10: Safety

Remember the old adage, "The apple doesn't fall far from the tree"? We often parent our kids the way *we* were parented, even if we are determined never to repeat the same patterns. It takes effort to remain conscious of actions, and that requires time for reflection. It helps kids feel empowered when they grow up in an environment where adults accept mistakes and encourage them to do their best.

·· ALWAYS
: ·· SOMETIMES
: : ·· NEVER

☐ ☐ ☐ I show my preteen that when I make mistakes, I try not to become angry with myself.

☐ ☐ ☐ I model patient responses to people who are new in their jobs (for instance, a new restaurant server or store clerk), and don't complain about their work in front of my preteen.

☐ ☐ ☐ When I was growing up, my family offered understanding, encouragement, and forgiveness when I or someone else in my house made a mistake.

☐ ☐ ☐ I offer my preteen the same understanding, encouragement, and forgiveness when he or she makes a mistake.

☐ ☐ ☐ When I struggled with a difficult task as a child, someone (a teacher, neighbor, relative, youth leader, or faith advisor) took time to help me see how I could do better. I seek out such mentors for my preteen.

☐ ☐ ☐ I model for my preteen a willingness to try new things at school, at home, or elsewhere without worrying about failing, and encourage my preteen to do the same.

☐ ☐ ☐ I help my preteen see mistakes as opportunities for learning.

☐ ☐ ☐ I offer my child opportunities to be a leader at home.

importance of the task at hand. Having too low a level of concern leads kids to underperform; too high a level of concern also leads kids to underperform.

Parents can determine appropriate expectations by closely observing and communicating with their children. Watch for indications of frustration or lack of effort. Gently inquire as to what is giving your preteens trouble. Remind them of their many prior successes and how they achieved them, often through patient practice.

At times it may be difficult to get your preteen to talk to you. Excellent resources on parent-child communication are available, including Adele Faber and Elaine Mazlish's *How to Talk So Kids Will Listen and Listen So Kids Will Talk* (1999), Charlene C. Giannetti and Margaret Sagarese's *The Roller Coaster Years* (1997), Ellen Rosenberg's *Get a Clue!* (1999), and Harriet S. Mosatche and Karen Unger's *Too Old for This, Too Young for That: Your Survival Guide for the Middle-School Years* (2000). These books can help you understand and address a variety of preteen issues (see "References" on page 169).

Building confidence is a process that begins early in children's lives. A parent's job is to make sure that children have many opportunities to accomplish specific tasks successfully so they build the confidence necessary to grow. If a child has developed adequate physical and cognitive maturity to handle various tasks, parents can then feel comfortable in expecting a certain level of competence.

For example, it's reasonable to ask your nine-year-old to set the table, as long as you have demonstrated how you expect the table to look. Accepting sloppy work doesn't help your preteen to feel empowered, although it may feel easier to you to set the table yourself rather than correct mistakes. By calmly restating your expectations and allowing your child an opportunity to do the task again, you send the message that you believe your child can do a competent job, as well as teach him an important life skill.

This message will carry over into other areas of your preteens' lives so that they know you are willing to support them in achieving your expectations. As they tackle more difficult academic tasks, they need to believe they can achieve success in order to keep trying.

Parents must walk a fine line between all sorts of unrealistic pressures in order to set realistic expectations. Most children want to be successful. When they are not, investigate and provide additional instruction or support to get your child back on track. Success leads to more success. When you offer your child an opportunity to be successful by gradually adding more demanding tasks (often unrelated to academics), this will have a positive impact on their academic success as well.

The Brain and Stress

Patricia Wolfe, Ed.D., author of *Brain Matters: Translating Research into Classroom Practice,* writes: "In the classroom, a student can perceive even a mild stressor to be threatening, initiating the stress response and lessening the student's ability to perform. You will probably have no difficulty enumerating some circumstances during which this can happen: being bullied or laughed at, taking part in timed testing, being called on when not prepared, or general fear of failure. Under these conditions, emotion is dominant over cognition, and the rational/thinking cortex is less efficient" (Wolfe, 2001).

Expect at the Correct Level of Expectation
To know whether your expectations for your preteen are appropriate, it is important to understand typical intellectual, physical, and emotional development. While young

Abstract Thinking and the Preteen

"Development of advanced mental processes, referred to as cognitive development, begins during early adolescence. Between the ages of 10 and 15, many people begin to develop the ability to think abstractly and reflectively. These new thinking abilities are called 'formal operations.' Since changes in thinking ability occur gradually, it is normal for a young adolescent to be able to think abstractly and reflectively in one area and to be tied to concrete thought in another. Although frustrating for adults, this is normal behavior for young adolescents. Important skills or information need to be conveyed in a variety of ways" (Center for Early Adolescence, 1992).

children think concretely, preteens begin to think more abstractly. Black-and-white thinking becomes grayer. Younger kids do well with a good deal of structure, while older kids are ready for more flexibility and choice. Additionally, remember that children develop according to their own unique timelines (see "References" on page 169).

! Parenting Tips: Building Empowered Preteens

Tip 1. Make mistakes safe to make.

In a busy world, it's easy to overreact, rather than to calmly respond to situations in a way that instructs your preteen how to better meet your expectations. Use mistakes as teaching opportunities to change preteen behavior in positive ways and develop your child's capacity for self-discipline. One idea? Make mistakes safe to make at home. Put a jar on the kitchen counter. If a family member makes an honest mistake, place a marble (penny or pebble) in the jar. When the jar is full, celebrate—go out for pizza, bake a special dessert, or better yet, ask the kids how they would like to celebrate. Think of how much more peaceful family life can be when you view honest mistakes as opportunities to improve, rather than as shortcomings to be punished.

Parent-child interactions might sound more like this: "Seems it's hard for you to remember to shut the front door so the dog won't get loose. How do you think you might remember to close it firmly so we don't have to go chasing her around the yard?" When kids become problem solvers, parents can become instructors, rather than frustrated gatekeepers. Or this: "Your teacher says you're not handing in your homework. That's going to affect your grade—and that's not okay. Let's think of three ways you can stay organized and get your work done on time. We'll write down your ideas and post them on the refrigerator. I'll help you in any way you want, because I know you can do this."

Tip 2. Teach, model, and practice the behavior you want to see.
Young people are usually eager to help others. So why not help your preteens see how they can contribute to the community by doing some service projects together? Parents who model volunteerism teach important values to their children and also show them how it is done.

Volunteering to cook and serve meals at a homeless shelter, collecting food or toiletries for an emergency food shelf, buying a holiday gift for a stranger, and assisting an elderly neighbor are all ways that families can work together to help children be community resources. As preteens learn what to do and how to do it, they can continue providing service to others on their own. They will learn life skills and develop confidence and empathy for others.

Tip 3. Be a partner in school success.

A preteen's work centers on school and includes both social and academic development. When it comes to schoolwork, stay on top of your child's progress and be prepared to help with organization, time management, and structure. Not all preteens need the same amount and kind of support when it comes to these three areas, but they all need some degree of help. Some use their time efficiently and stay on top of assignments at an early age; others need more time to develop those skills.

In general, boys need more time than girls to develop effective organizational skills. Provide the appropriate support based on individual needs and personality for as long as it is needed. It might be tempting to give up in frustration, but rather than saying "By this time, you should be able to do this without my reminding you," stick with your child to help him or her develop more effective strategies. Eventually, they *will* remember on their own.

Because preteens struggle with the tension between industry and inferiority (as Erik Erikson argued), this is not the time to let them sink or swim. I remember being told to let my son suffer the consequences of his inability to organize himself, allowing him to fail so that he would learn the hard way. I'm glad I rejected that advice. I knew intuitively that if I stopped supporting my struggling preteen, he would experience the failure and frustration that could lead to giving up or seeing himself as incapable or less than his peers.

When I made this decision, I knew how hard my son was trying in school. He clearly wanted to do well, but was having trouble. If he had not been so motivated to try, and merely ignored deadlines, then perhaps letting him experience the consequences of his actions would have been helpful. I preferred to provide additional support until he could assume the tasks alone. Every parent must take an honest look at his or her child and determine the best course of action. No one knows your child better than you do.

Kids who believe they are capable of achieving a goal will keep trying; but those who do not believe in themselves give up. Do everything in your power to ensure your preteens achieve some level of success so that they have a base to build upon. Organizational skills improve with maturity, time, and patient instruction and support.

Despite your best efforts, occasionally a child may spurn your help with schoolwork. Some insist they have things under control when you can see that is not the case. Rely on hard data and resist getting pulled into verbal disputes. Monitoring report cards and test scores is one way to gather data. If grades and tests scores begin to slip, it is best to intervene quickly without waiting for the next report card.

Kids in middle childhood sometimes stretch limits and try to be more independent than they are capable of being. It is reasonable to expect your preteens to show you their grades and progress notes on assignments, tests, and projects. It is also a good idea to require preteens to spend a designated amount of time on homework, studying, or reading each school night. If they refuse or repeatedly insist they have no homework or studying to do, confirm this with teachers.

Many schools require teachers to post homework assignments on their Web sites. Other schools set up homework hotlines so that students and parents can access assignments. Most teachers welcome e-mails from parents and students. You can also call teachers at school and inquire about your preteen's progress and effort. You may be reassured that all is well. But if not, you and the teacher can work with your preteen to do better.

As your preteen demonstrates increasingly responsible behavior, you can expand your boundaries. Remember to rely on the facts (grades, tests, and teacher comments). Negotiating based on a "feeling" level is not productive. You'll likely get comments such as "You don't trust me" or "You don't understand." When you stick to the data, usually the emotional level decreases, and you can set clear, reasonable expectations for achievement.

Tip 4. Use discipline techniques wisely.
Making mistakes safe to make can be tricky. There are fine lines separating having high expectations, making mistakes safe to make, and being too lenient. Parents need to show common sense and good judgment. Remember the puddle? If you were to punish excessively or react harshly to a mistake or rule infraction, it would be like throwing a very big rock into a puddle. The puddle would be diminished, and you never want discipline to diminish your child in any way.

On the other hand, ignoring mistakes and infractions in order to keep the peace is like throwing such a small pebble into the puddle that the puddle is not disturbed at all. This teaches a child nothing. To be most effective, provide consequences that fit the situation, are enforceable, and teach the lesson the child needs to learn. Think before you react. Give your preteen (and yourself) a time out or cooling off period so you can really consider your response and make sure it is appropriate. You may want to consult your spouse, parenting partner, or trusted friend for their perspective before you take corrective action. It is helpful to let preteens contemplate the issue and reflect on the consequences of their actions.

Tip 5. Watch out for parent traps.
Teach your child early the difference between making an honest mistake and neglecting responsibility. Kids know the difference. It does them no good if you are lenient

when they choose to avoid work or other responsibilities. It's an honest mistake when a preteen puts too much detergent in the dishwasher and ends up with suds on the floor. But it is neglect of responsibilities when he watches TV instead of doing an assigned chore like dishwashing.

In the case of the child who winds up with suds all over the floor, you have a range of reactions to choose from. You can react with exasperation, or you can laugh with your child over the mistake, show him the correct amount of detergent to use, and then clean up the mess together. What a great way to build a relationship, too. Remember, it's your choice as to how you will react.

When a child neglects responsibility, an appropriate consequence might include a one-on-one conversation. Discuss the importance of being a dependable member of the family whose contributions are expected and appreciated. Taking away a valued privilege for a day or two is also appropriate.

Additional Thoughts for Empowering Kids

It helps to believe that people (your preteen included) generally want to do the right thing. If they make mistakes, it's usually because they lack the skills, judgment, or support to do better. Start by sitting down with your child and having a direct and honest conversation. Share your own experiences as a kid and show her the questions that helped you reflect on your own behavior. Your child may reflect on her own actions, too, and begin the process of breaking the old cycle.

The next time your child makes a mistake, ask yourself, "Under what circumstances would I have done the same thing?" Often, there is a reasonable explanation for a child's decision. Remember that preteens are not as capable as adults of thinking through the consequences of their decisions. Things make sense to them at the time, and they often do not foresee all of the possibilities that can result from a given action. Add the element of peer involvement to some of these actions, and you can see why kids get themselves into jams.

Preteens are works in progress. Their brains will not be fully capable of reflection, problem solving, and organization until their mid-twenties. New techniques for studying the brain confirm that adolescent brains function very differently than adult brains. Jay Geidd, M.D., an expert in brain development at the National Institute of Mental Health in Bethesda, Maryland, says that adults use their prefrontal cortex to make decisions, while adolescents process decisions in the emotional centers of the brain (see "Online Resources" on page 173). Youth think with their hearts and guts. If you ask them, "What were you thinking?" they may answer that they *weren't* thinking—at least not in the way adults do. That's why they need you to set reasonable boundaries and clear expectations for them.

BOUNDARIES AND EXPECTATIONS

Safety nets—trapeze artists can't learn their trade without them. Kids need them, too. Boundaries and expectations are safety nets. They provide the structure and safety for preteens to learn and function in their worlds. Without boundaries, kids do not know how far they can go in social or school situations before they find themselves in over their heads. To be effective, parents need to create boundaries and expectations that flex and grow as children mature. Setting boundaries and expectations at a level that's appropriate for your preteen's development can be a tricky proposition.

Being able to think through consequences is not easy for preteens, and as a result, they can be impulsive. Preteens don't typically worry about negative consequences, since they believe they are invincible. They

Spotlight on the Boundaries-and-Expectations Assets

A boy becomes an adult three years before his parents think he does, and about two years after he thinks he does. **LEWIS HERSHEY, 1951**

Search Institute identifies the six Boundaries-and-Expectations assets as follows:

11. Family boundaries
12. School boundaries
13. Neighborhood boundaries
14. Adult role models
15. Positive peer influence
16. High expectations

organize and respond to information according to their developmental level. Therefore, preteens need role models and structure far longer than they think they do.

Preteens often challenge rules that they feel no longer apply to them. This can be frustrating for parents. "Because I said so" probably doesn't work as well with preteens as it did when they were preschoolers. Preteens are beginning to think differently. They no longer regard all issues as black or white, good or bad, safe or unsafe. They are now beginning to notice gray areas that are situation-specific.

Preteens also notice inconsistencies and differences between your rules and other parents' rules. Children at this stage are very concerned with justice and fairness. They need to understand the reasoning behind the rules in order to follow them. Your child may challenge you, and you may have to work harder to ensure that you back up your rules with logical reasoning.

Being flexible is key. Involve your preteen in discussions and negotiations about rules, curfews, movies and music, expectations for behavior, appropriate dress, and so on. Doing this is hard work and may explain why so many parents begin to feel worn down or anxious over the approaching teen years. However, this is when you begin to draw on your "relationship account." An appropriate sense of humor can go a long way in defusing tensions between your preteen and you. If you keep a positive perspective and understand (even celebrate) your child's cognitive development, the preteen years can be good for both of you.

What's Up with the Preteen Brain?

Author and educator Kathie F. Nunley, Ed.D., explains, "[Young people] appear to have at least three strikes against them when it comes to using logic to weigh the risks in dangerous or sometimes even everyday types of decisions. The more primitive regions of their brains are strong and tend to drive behaviors. The immature region responsible for the logic of long-term benefits does not always override the impulsive, survival-oriented hypothalamus. Add any additional trauma to the mix, such as abusive households or drug and alcohol use, and the issue becomes even more severe. . . . Time and good role models will fortunately allow the brain to eventually mature to match the body" (Nunley, help4teachers.com).

❗ *Parenting Tips: Providing Boundaries and Expectations*

Tip 1. Respect preteens' new cognitive abilities.

Preteens want to be seen as the emerging adults that they are. You can demonstrate your respect for their new abilities by adapting rules as a team. Convey the mes-

ASSET 11: Family Boundaries
ASSET 12: School Boundaries
ASSET 13: Neighborhood Boundaries
ASSET 14: Adult Role Models
ASSET 15: Positive Peer Influence
ASSET 16: High Expectations

Reflection and Discussion:
Boundaries and Expectations

Think about how you are doing when it comes to providing your child with boundaries and expectations. Use these statements as the basis for actions you can take to enhance this asset area for your preteen.

· · ALWAYS
: · · SOMETIES
: : · · NEVER

☐ ☐ ☐ I provide my preteen with structure that offers choice (for example, "You seem to have a couple of hours of homework a day. Would you like to do it right after school, or take a break and do it after dinner?").

☐ ☐ ☐ I provide my child with a rationale for my rules and stand my ground when other parents have different rules and expectations for their preteens.

☐ ☐ ☐ I talk openly about my own values and behavior.

☐ ☐ ☐ I am clear about my expectations for my preteen's behavior, and I check to see if my child understands me.

☐ ☐ ☐ I know the parents of my child's friends and talk about our family rules with other parents.

☐ ☐ ☐ I'm comfortable making tough decisions even if my preteen gets angry with me.

☐ ☐ ☐ My kids know they can use me as an excuse when they have to say no to friends who want to do something risky.

☐ ☐ ☐ When my kids misbehave, I follow through with appropriate consequences.

☐ ☐ ☐ I am consistent and fair in the way I treat my preteen.

☐ ☐ ☐ I open my home to my preteen's friends, making them feel welcome, safe, and cared for, and I hold them to high standards of behavior as I do my own child.

sage that when everyone in the family works together as a team, more gets accomplished. When your preteen is ready for more responsibility, discuss your expectations. If she is old enough to walk to school or ride her bike with friends to the park, talk about the issue at a family meeting.

But remember that your main responsibility is to instruct and protect your child. Make an appointment to meet where you can talk on neutral turf. Bring your issues and some paper to write on and create a written agreement that you can both live with and refer to later. Respect your preteen's opinions. Take all ideas into account and compromise where possible.

Tip 2. Teach preteens how to get out of sticky situations.
It is one thing to expect your kids to resist negative peer pressure, but it is another to teach them how to resist that pressure. Role-play possible scenarios that they might face. Brainstorm possible answers they could give to kids who are pressuring them to do something they know is wrong. Make sure they understand that you are willing to be their biggest excuse. Tell them, for example, that they could say, "Are you kidding? My mom would be really mad if I did that. I would be grounded for a year! Sorry, but I have to pass."

Tip 3. Make your home one that kids want to come to.
Open your house to your preteen's friends, and make it a safe, fun place to gather. Express your expectations for their behavior, such as no throwing balls inside or no jumping on furniture, keep food out of the living room, no profanities in our house, and clean up any messes you make. Most kids respect other parents' rules.

Don't let your children talk you into becoming invisible to spare them the embarrassment of having you around. Greet friends by name, ask them how they are doing, what's new in their lives, and how their families are. Then allow them to go where they can be together. However, it is a good idea to show up unexpectedly (with food or drinks) and check in.

Let your child's friends know you care about what they are doing. If things get rowdy, be calm but firm in re-establishing order. If you cannot, then ask them to leave with the understanding that they are always welcome to return when they can respect your rules.

Tip 4. Meet the parents of your preteen's friends.
Make it a priority to get to know other parents. It is a good way to learn about other people's standards and expectations. When your older preteen wants to go with friends to a movie or the mall without you, call other parents and agree on pick-up times, movie choices, and their availability in the area. Other parents appreciate being called and sharing their expectations for their children's behavior, too.

One day your child will learn to drive, and if you've become comfortable regularly checking in with other parents, you can readily join forces with them at this risky time to enforce curfews and driving rules. Parents need the support of other parents to provide safety nets for all their kids.

CONSTRUCTIVE USE OF TIME

How preteens spend their spare time is critical during this stage of development. It's important that preteens have opportunities to use their out-of-school time to develop their passions, interests, and skills; discover new ideas; and have some unstructured time at home to play, rest, and recharge.

During early adolescence, around the ages of 11 to 12 years, the brain undergoes two processes known

Spotlight on the
Constructive-Use-of-Time Assets

Search Institute researchers have discovered that a number
of activities help young people develop into successful,
healthy adults. These are the Constructive-Use-of-Time assets,
which include:

17. Creative activities
18. Child programs
19. Religious community
20. Time at home

as "blossoming" and "pruning." Blossoming is the
huge growth spurt of dendrites (nerve cell endings
that receive information and transmit nerve impulses).
Pruning removes dendrites that are not used (or hard-
wired) into the brain. Experience causes the brain to
activate neurons (nerve cells). When the neurons are
activated over and over, they become hard-wired in
the brain. The hard wiring indicates that a person has
developed a skill.

Experience continually molds a young person's
brain, so what adolescents do with their time is extremely
important. Jay Geidd, M.D., of the National Institute of
Mental Health in Bethesda, Maryland, hypothesizes that
the growth of the thinking part of the brain, followed by
the pruning of connections, is a particularly important
stage of brain development. The way teens spend their
time can affect them for the rest of their lives. Geidd calls
this the "use it or lose it" principle (www.pbs.org).

As preteens participate in sports, music, and other
activities; develop social skills; and learn new things, neural connections blossom and become hard-wired in the
brain. Therefore, constructive use of time is more than a

good idea. It is a necessity for healthy social, emotional, and cognitive development.

At various stages of development, the brain experiences "open windows" of opportunity. For example, the window of opportunity for phonemic awareness (noticing and distinguishing the blending of letter combinations when spoken) is wide open during the first three years of life. This is how babies develop language. This window gradually closes around age 12 and explains why children learn languages so easily when compared to adults.

For adolescents, open windows of opportunity "relate to the wiring of impulse control, relationships, and communication. That's why," says psychologist David Walsh, Ph.D., "parents need to pay attention when preteens spend hours playing violent video games while their window of opportunity to develop healthy relationships is open wide. It also makes sense to encourage adolescents to get involved with service projects and volunteer opportunities while brain circuits related to social relationships are blossoming and pruning" (Walsh, 2004).

❗ Parenting Tips: Encouraging Constructive Use of Time

Tip 1. Practice what you preach.
Why not ask your preteen what novels or other literature he or she is reading in school, and then read those books as well? Your kids will benefit from hearing your perspective on what you did and did not like, and you will be modeling a constructive use of time for them.

Tip 2. Competitive sports aren't for everyone.
Not all children are interested in playing competitive team sports nor necessarily benefit from playing games they dislike. Instead, encourage your preteen to enjoy individual physical activities like skiing, skateboarding,

ASSET 17: Creative Activities
ASSET 18: Child Programs
ASSET 19: Religious Community
ASSET 20: Time at Home

Do you provide constructive experiences for your child and monitor your child's use of free time? Consider these statements, and choose one or two to use as prompts for positive action and discussion with your preteen.

- ALWAYS
  - SOMETIMES
    - NEVER

☐ ☐ ☐ I encourage my child to participate in music, sports, drama, or other worthwhile after-school activities.

☐ ☐ ☐ I look for ways to provide after-school options for my preteen in addition to sports or music (for example, chess club, scrapbooking, cooking, sledding, bowling, skating, hiking, fishing, or movies).

☐ ☐ ☐ Our family participates in faith community programs or services at least once a week.

☐ ☐ ☐ I expect my preteen to be at home on school nights doing homework (unless school-related activities are going on).

☐ ☐ ☐ My child gets enough sleep each night (at least eight to nine hours). I have a "lights-out" time and consistently enforce it, except on special occasions.

☐ ☐ ☐ I model healthy eating and exercise habits for my preteen, and my preteen eats a balanced diet and gets regular exercise.

☐ ☐ ☐ I limit the number of hours my child plays computer or video games and monitor the types of games that are played.

☐ ☐ ☐ I don't allow my preteen to have a computer or TV in the bedroom.

☐ ☐ ☐ I monitor my child's use of Web sites, instant messaging, text messaging, and cell phones.

bike riding, fishing, and skating if traditional team sports are not their thing. Be available to provide transportation for your preteen and his or her friends. Kids need interactions with their peers to develop social competence.

Look for alternate opportunities to gather kids together, especially shy preteens who need extra encouragement. Scrapbooking, photography, birdwatching, and cartooning are all good possibilities. When preteens need additional time and encouragement to feel comfortable with their peers, these activities keep their hands busy and allow them to relax, start conversations, and share their creations. Other opportunities to get kids talking to one another and acquiring valuable social skills include building forts, cooking, going fishing, and taking group hikes.

Tip 3. Relax together.

If you meet resistance from your preteen about restricting TV viewing, set aside a special time each week to watch one of his or her favorite shows and share a treat together. Talk about the characters and plot. Ask why the program is appealing. Comment on what you see. Share time together in other pastimes, including reading, working on favorite collections, or listening to music. The main point is to join your preteen in spending relaxing time together!

COMMITMENT TO LEARNING

If kids stop enjoying learning or do not find meaning in what they are learning, they'll eventually lack academic commitment. If your preteen isn't showing a commitment to learning, investigate the reasons. The way you model your own lifelong learning, the way you react to mistakes that your kids make, and the way they perceive their abilities, and school climate all contribute to their commitment to learning.

Spotlight on the Commitment-to-Learning Assets

The Search Institute defines the five Commitment-to-Learning assets as follows:

21. Achievement motivation
22. Learning engagement
23. Homework
24. Bonding to school
25. Reading for pleasure

❗ *Parenting Tips: Enhancing Commitment to Learning*

Tip 1. Teach your kids how to get organized.

Preteen brains are beginning to develop a capacity for the sophisticated tasks of decision making, reflection, and organization. Providing a daily planner is a good first step toward helping them stay on top of their tasks. The next step is teaching them to use the planner and then monitoring its use. Rather than checking it daily, let your preteens know that you will be checking it at random. Make sure they know you expect them to keep the planner up-to-date. Set a consequence if they don't (for example, no TV that night after homework is done). Be consistent. It may take awhile for some kids to develop the habit of using an organizer or daily planner. Stay alongside your kids and support their growing organizational skills.

Tip 2. Teach long-range planning skills.

Given the busy pace of preteens' lives, they need to be able to plan ahead and budget their time. You can help your child learn that skill by monitoring her planner and

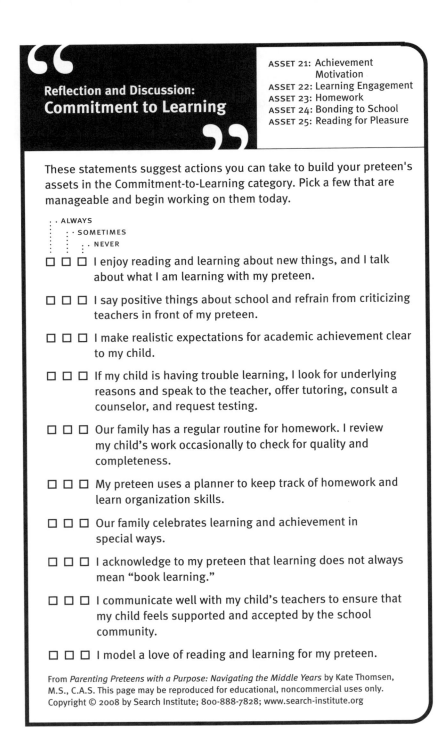

Reflection and Discussion:
Commitment to Learning

ASSET 21: Achievement Motivation
ASSET 22: Learning Engagement
ASSET 23: Homework
ASSET 24: Bonding to School
ASSET 25: Reading for Pleasure

These statements suggest actions you can take to build your preteen's assets in the Commitment-to-Learning category. Pick a few that are manageable and begin working on them today.

. . ALWAYS
. . · SOMETIMES
. . . . NEVER

☐ ☐ ☐ I enjoy reading and learning about new things, and I talk about what I am learning with my preteen.

☐ ☐ ☐ I say positive things about school and refrain from criticizing teachers in front of my preteen.

☐ ☐ ☐ I make realistic expectations for academic achievement clear to my child.

☐ ☐ ☐ If my child is having trouble learning, I look for underlying reasons and speak to the teacher, offer tutoring, consult a counselor, and request testing.

☐ ☐ ☐ Our family has a regular routine for homework. I review my child's work occasionally to check for quality and completeness.

☐ ☐ ☐ My preteen uses a planner to keep track of homework and learn organization skills.

☐ ☐ ☐ Our family celebrates learning and achievement in special ways.

☐ ☐ ☐ I acknowledge to my preteen that learning does not always mean "book learning."

☐ ☐ ☐ I communicate well with my child's teachers to ensure that my child feels supported and accepted by the school community.

☐ ☐ ☐ I model a love of reading and learning for my preteen.

asking questions about long-term assignments. Here's how it might sound:

Parent: So, you have a project to do in social studies class.

Preteen: Yeah, but it isn't due for a long time. I'm not worried about it now.

Parent: Do you have a plan for doing it?

Preteen: Well, I'll do it when the time gets closer.

Parent: Is this a project that involves going to the library?

Preteen: Yeah.

Parent: When would you like to do that? Have you thought about what you need to read and what supplies we should gather? Is your project a paper, a presentation, or a diorama?

As you ask questions, your child begins to conceptualize the project. She begins to narrow the scope of the project and think about what she has to do. Keep going.

Preteen: Well, our teacher gave us a choice, and I can choose what I want to do.

Parent: Okay, but you still have other homework and activities during this time, don't you? How about we get out the calendar and plan when you might get some of this done?

Getting kids to talk through the sequence of activities for completing a project is a great way to teach planning skills. Encourage preteens to make a "To Do" list with dates to accomplish each task. Outline steps for a project to make it more manageable. If the project seems overwhelming, kids often procrastinate and do a poor job. Long-range planning skills, like breaking a task into smaller parts, making a list, and creating a time line are skills they can use for life. When preteens realize these skills give them tools for success, they will stay interested in and committed to their projects.

Tip 3. Encourage all kinds of interests.

Preteens develop interests in many areas. Unless those interests are harmful, be careful not to be judgmental. Kids become easily discouraged when they perceive negativity from adults they care about. When I was training to become a teacher, I remember believing that reading comic books wasn't as valuable as reading the classics. I later learned that reading is *reading*. The more a person reads and enjoys what he reads, the better reader he or she becomes. Using comic books or graphic novels with basic literary integrity to teach plot and character development works just as well as using a novel.

Steven Covey, author of *The Seven Habits of Highly Effective People* (1990), urges: "Seek first to understand, and then to be understood." If kids have a particular interest, uncover what it is about the topic that appeals to them. Use their interests to establish rapport. Ask them to teach you more about an area they like. You may be surprised at their perspectives and depth of knowledge.

Very often, schools are bound by far too many standards and requirements to encourage student learning based on individual interests. This is where parents come in. With an open mind, you can encourage all kinds of worthwhile interests in your child. Sometimes, success in an activity outside of school helps a child experience success within school. Success breeds success, and there's nothing else like it.

POSITIVE VALUES

Values drive our behavior, because we act on what we believe in. If we believe that something has value, don't we take measures to protect it? Our values are no different. We naturally want to protect the values that we believe in. One way to protect our values is to pass them on to our children.

Spotlight on the Positive-Values Assets

Search Institute names the following character qualities the Positive-Values assets:

26. Caring
27. Equality and social justice
28. Integrity
29. Honesty
30. Responsibility
31. Healthy lifestyle

Earlier, you thought about the people (and experiences) that contributed to making you the person you are today. Each shared their values with you through example, instruction, and discipline. They may not even have realized their influence at the time. Values are conveyed openly through discussion, instruction, and role modeling. But values also are conveyed through inaction and silence. Reflect on some of the ways that you communicate your values to your children.

Parenting Tips: Instilling Positive Values

Tip 1. Actions speak louder than words.
Kids do not miss a trick when it comes to watching parents, so make sure you do what you say. Wear your seat belt, eat healthy food, don't smoke. Model the behaviors you wish to see in your kids. If you are single and dating, be aware that your sexual behavior sets the standard in your home. If you are married or in a committed partnership, be aware that your behavior toward your partner influences how your children behave in their own relationships with others.

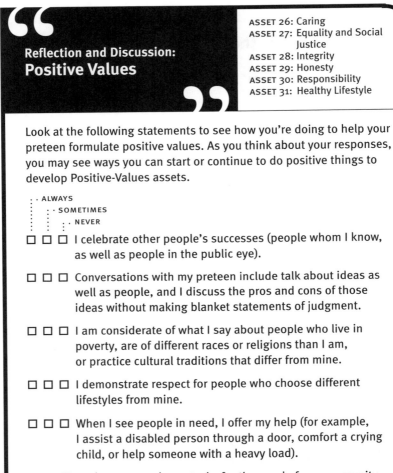

Reflection and Discussion:
Positive Values

ASSET 26: Caring
ASSET 27: Equality and Social Justice
ASSET 28: Integrity
ASSET 29: Honesty
ASSET 30: Responsibility
ASSET 31: Healthy Lifestyle

Look at the following statements to see how you're doing to help your preteen formulate positive values. As you think about your responses, you may see ways you can start or continue to do positive things to develop Positive-Values assets.

· · ALWAYS
· · · SOMETIMES
· · · · NEVER

☐ ☐ ☐ I celebrate other people's successes (people whom I know, as well as people in the public eye).

☐ ☐ ☐ Conversations with my preteen include talk about ideas as well as people, and I discuss the pros and cons of those ideas without making blanket statements of judgment.

☐ ☐ ☐ I am considerate of what I say about people who live in poverty, are of different races or religions than I am, or practice cultural traditions that differ from mine.

☐ ☐ ☐ I demonstrate respect for people who choose different lifestyles from mine.

☐ ☐ ☐ When I see people in need, I offer my help (for example, I assist a disabled person through a door, comfort a crying child, or help someone with a heavy load).

☐ ☐ ☐ I volunteer to take on tasks for the good of my community.

☐ ☐ ☐ I listen to others even when I disagree, and try to understand the other person's point of view.

☐ ☐ ☐ I encourage my preteen to express opinions without fearing ridicule from siblings or other adults, and I make sure it's safe in my home to stand up for personal beliefs.

☐ ☐ ☐ I assign my preteen chores that are necessary for the effective running of our home and expect that they will be done.

Tip 2. Get involved in your community.

Sometimes preteens cannot appreciate what they have *because* they are preteens! Educate your children about the disparity between wants and needs. Help them to understand what they have and foster a belief in helping those who are less fortunate. Teach them about the work of social service agencies, such as local food shelves and how they help the community. Ask them to help clean out closets and donate outgrown clothes or toys to the organization of their choice. Kids can also contribute a canned good or paper product once a week to a box you provide. When it's full, deliver it together to the food pantry.

Tip 3. Use community resources.

Most communities have a wealth of organizations that can enhance the development of a young person's skills, interests, empathy, and competencies. The YMCA offers healthy, cost-effective youth programming options for recreation and social development. The YMCA embraces the concept of positive youth development and integrates opportunities for youth voices in programming and planning. City park and recreation departments, 4-H clubs and faith communities are also rich in youth programs that offer youth opportunities to contribute to their community. Organizations such as Big Brothers Big Sisters of America assist youth in connecting with other caring adults when parents are not able to meet all of their children's needs. Habitat for Humanity and the Red Cross offer young people opportunities to work and contribute their time and skills for the benefit of others. The list is long and also includes familiar clubs such as the Boy Scouts and Girl Scouts, Boys and Girls Clubs of America, Campfire USA, and others.

Encouraging your preteens to get involved in healthy activities outside the home helps them to develop a broader awareness of people from different cultures and backgrounds and the social skills to interact with others respectfully. As preteens deepen their understanding of the world around them, they begin to understand themselves and their capabilities better. This cognitive awareness helps preteens to be more resilient when facing various life challenges.

Tip 4. Follow the news together.
Newspapers and news shows offer a tremendous resource for discussing social justice topics. National, international, and local stories about need, injustice, and civic responsibility are there for the taking. How about choosing one night a week to discuss a newspaper article or news program that caught your attention? Ask your child to pick a story too. Learning about each other's perspectives can be enriching for both of you. And, together you might discuss ways to take action toward making the world a better place.

SOCIAL COMPETENCIES

The Social-Competencies assets are critical ingredients in a young person's ability to manage feelings and emotions, make competent decisions, and interact with people in socially successful ways. Author Daniel Goleman calls this set of skills "emotional intelligence" in his book *Emotional Intelligence: Why It Can Matter More Than IQ* (1995). He argues that a lack of emotional intelligence can mean the difference between success and failure for a person, regardless of IQ. In fact, Goleman believes that emotional intelligence is, at times, even more powerful than intellectual capacity. The Social-Competencies assets center on this ability to know and manage our emotions and interactions with others and to make good decisions.

Spotlight on the Social-Competencies Assets

Preteens are learning and refining many social skills. These are the five Social Competencies that Search Institute researchers have identified as Developmental Assets for preteens:

32. Planning and decision making
33. Interpersonal competence
34. Cultural competence
35. Resistance skills
36. Peaceful conflict resolution

Social competence develops through trial and error, as well as by observing competent role models. Preteens learn to become socially competent primarily from watching their parents. But it's important to let your kids know that as they try new and different things, you're available to help talk through the uncertainties.

❶ Parenting Tips: Building Social Competencies

Tip 1. Teach kids to identify feelings.
Sometimes it takes a while even for adults to understand how they feel at a given moment. You may discover at times that you are actually sad when you thought you were angry. Kids, too, need help accurately identifying their emotions to deal effectively with their feelings. Preteens often seem angry when they really are hurt. If your child is upset, first allow a period of time alone. Then quietly ask what is wrong and gently probe for details. You can rephrase this information to your child to help understand and identify feelings. Together, you can begin to devise ways to deal with the issue.

Reflection and Discussion:
Social Competencies

ASSET 32: Planning and Decision Making
ASSET 33: Interpersonal Competence
ASSET 34: Cultural Competence
ASSET 35: Resistance Skills
ASSET 36: Peaceful Conflict Resolution

Take a look at the following statements to see how you're doing at helping your preteen develop the Social-Competencies assets. Begin by reflecting on your own actions so far. Look for ways to start or continue doing positive things that support your preteen's growing social competence.

· · ALWAYS
    · · SOMETIMES
       · · NEVER

☐ ☐ ☐ I take time to teach my kids how to be courteous: to shake hands, make eye contact, speak politely, give and receive compliments, say thank you or express appreciation, and answer the telephone appropriately.

☐ ☐ ☐ I consistently offer my preteen the opportunity to participate in making decisions and plans that affect the family.

☐ ☐ ☐ I talk to my child about the factors I consider when I make a decision (for example, short-term benefits vs. long-term effects of a particular decision or the financial feasibility of various choices).

☐ ☐ ☐ I teach simple tools for decision making, such as listing pros and cons of an idea, or looking at an issue or decision from other points of view.

☐ ☐ ☐ I encourage my child to learn about and value other cultures' customs and traditions.

☐ ☐ ☐ I express my appreciation of other people's traditions and lifestyles.

☐ ☐ ☐ I have talked with my preteen about how to say no when he or she feels pressured to do something that is wrong.

☐ ☐ ☐ In our house, people feel safe to disagree, and we focus on resolving conflict peacefully.

When preteens are upset or stressed, it is also helpful to teach them where they feel the emotion in their bodies. Stomachs and heads are often the places where "upsets" land. Having that information can be a useful tool so that when stomachs feel tight or heads begin to ache, children can think about what is going on and identify the source of their stress. They can then do something to change the way they feel.

Tip 2. Teach healthy stress relievers.

Stress causes the body to produce chemicals (such as cortisol, a hormone secreted by the adrenal gland) that can be harmful over the long term. No one likes feeling stressed or upset. Sometimes people try to alleviate stress in unhealthy ways, using food, shopping, sex, alcohol, or drugs. There are better ways to produce the beneficial chemicals (endorphins) that can change feelings. Teach your child through your actions how to feel better and manage feelings in positive ways. Exercise, sports, yoga, talking, walking, listening to music, meditating, volunteering, praying, and other healthy outlets all can help relieve stress.

Tip 3. Make it OK to have feelings.

As preteens move toward age 11 or 12, they embark on a roller coaster ride of new emotions and feelings. You may not always understand the quick changes that you witness, but you don't really have to. Chances are, your preteen won't always know what triggers her ups and downs either. Your child may start the day happy and carefree and return three hours later, depressed and burdened.

Your job is to acknowledge your child's feelings and react appropriately. Join in her joy, celebrate the happy hours, and gently offer hugs and opportunities to talk when the sad hours arrive. When you show you are aware of your preteen's feelings and that you care about what she's feeling, she's more likely to show appreciation toward you. Refrain from making statements like, "What in the world do you have to be so upset about?" or "Just get over it and put a smile on your face." Neither of these statements acknowledges the right to having feelings, and neither one is particularly helpful to your child. Instead of saying, "I know how you feel," substitute comforting words like, "Tell me how you feel."

Tip 4. Offer opportunities for nonverbal communication.
One way to offer children the opportunity to communicate to the family without using words is to place a large thermometer (made from simple materials like cardboard) in the kitchen. They move a marker along the thermometer to a place that communicates how they're feeling. Low placement means a bad day, high placement means a great day, and so on. You can monitor the thermometer and get a "heads-up" for the kind of interactions you might have with your child. This technique works especially well when your child has difficulty making the transition from one setting to another (coming home from school or another activity, for instance).

Help preteens consider the state of their feelings and communicate that information to you. Clear communication is an invaluable skill throughout life. Giving each member of the family a different colored marker allows you to monitor how each person is feeling. This technique allows family members to develop empathy for others' feelings and experiences.

Tip 5. Teach ways to resolve conflict.
Marriage and family counselors use a conflict resolution technique called "fair fighting." You can adapt this method for use with your preteen. Here are the main steps:

- *Be respectful.* No put-downs or sarcasm, and no hurtful statements.

- *Keep the problem as the focus.* Don't turn a person into the problem. Use "I" statements and state clearly how you feel.

- *Stay on one subject.* Don't bring in other problems.

- *Use time-outs as needed.* If tempers flare, call a time-out and meet back later.

- *Listen for understanding.* Consider the other person's point of view to be as important as yours.

- *Don't try to mind-read.* Don't assume that you know what the other person is thinking.

- *Seek to solve the problem.* Say, "What can we do together to solve this?"

- *Forgive and accept each other.* Remember, disagreements are shared (www.positive-way.com).

Listen to each side and ask what each person is responsible for and what they might have done differently. If you practice these steps with your preteen when conflicts arise, you will solve problems more effectively, as well as teach this valuable skill to your child.

POSITIVE IDENTITY

One of the markers for resilient people is having a positive view of the future (Benard, 1991). People who believe they have a bright future are more likely to resist negative peer pressure and make good decisions about their personal behaviors. Having a sense of personal power, high self-esteem, a sense of purpose, and a belief in a positive future all fuel a person's creativity and

Spotlight on the Positive-Identity Assets

A strong personal identity is more than just high self-esteem.
Search Institute researchers define the Positive-Identity assets
as follows:

37. Personal power
38. Self-esteem
39. Sense of purpose
40. Positive view of personal future

motivation. For preteens with these assets, the world is a
friendly place full of exciting challenges and opportunities that are within their reach.

Parenting Tips: Building Positive Identity

Tip 1. Celebrate rites of passage.

As younger children become preteens, they will experience typical rites of passage, including the transition from
elementary to middle school, landing a part in the school
play, attending a school dance, having a first menstrual
cycle, and perhaps growing taller than you! Let your
child know that you notice his milestones. Celebrating
these big events acknowledges his progress through the
preteen years and communicates the value you place
on his age-appropriate accomplishments. Document his
successes with photos, words, special meals, or other
ways that acknowledge your preteen's growth and
achievements.

Tip 2. Begin future visioning.

It may be a bit overwhelming to young people to think
about what they will do with their lives in the future

66

Reflection and Discussion:
Positive Identity

ASSET 37: Personal Power
ASSET 38: Self-esteem
ASSET 39: Sense of Purpose
ASSET 40: Positive View of
Personal Future

99

Read through the following statements to see how you're doing at supporting your preteen's growing positive identity. Think about your responses and look for ways to continue supporting the development of your preteen's Positive-Identity assets.

- ALWAYS
  - SOMETIMES
    - NEVER

□ □ □ I allow my child to participate in making family decisions.

□ □ □ I teach my preteen how to make good decisions regarding alcohol and other drug use.

□ □ □ I am willing to consider my preteen's point of view on issues related to fairness, equality, and justice.

□ □ □ My preteen considers others' points of view.

□ □ □ My preteen expresses pride in her or his accomplishments.

□ □ □ I demonstrate to my preteen that all people deserve respect and understanding.

□ □ □ My preteen and I discuss ways he or she might contribute to society as adults.

□ □ □ My kids and I talk about their future plans for education and work.

□ □ □ I am optimistic about my child's future.

□ □ □ My preteen is also optimistic about her or his own future.

because the choices are so vast. Preteens often first consider holding the jobs that those closest to them have. The preteen years are a good time to start discussing future vocations.

Whenever possible, point out various jobs and careers that may appeal to your kids. Encourage them to picture themselves doing a particular job, and talk about what is and is not appealing to them. Avoid judging their comments. When you visit a garden center, ask your kids whether landscaping appeals to them. How about jobs held by building designers? Carpenters? Chefs? Journalists? Asking questions now encourages your children to consider future possibilities. Let them know you believe they can do anything they set their sights on.

Encourage children to research occupations that interest them on the Internet and at the library. Find out the qualifications for particular jobs. Don't expect kids to stick with one choice. The idea at this age is to explore and envision the future. The more possibilities children imagine for themselves at this stage, the better.

An effective way to help preteens begin envisioning their future is to encourage them to participate in intergenerational activities with other adults. A mentoring relationship allows an adult to invest in a young person's success and offer guidance and understanding. Mentors can often see and nurture aspects of a child that are different from the ones a parent focuses on.

Some mentoring programs, like Big Brothers Big Sisters of America, require a long-term commitment to building a relationship and providing opportunities for a child. Other mentoring programs are structured around specific activities, such as volunteering at a nature center or helping at an animal shelter. The mentoring is specific to the activity and occurs when the activity takes place.

Some schools offer service learning (also called experiential learning or problem-based learning) as part of the curriculum (see "Online Resources" on page 173). Service learning offers students the opportunity to connect what they're learning in the classroom to solving real problems in the community (such as planning and creating public gardens, supporting people living in poverty, or cleaning polluted areas). Students learn from adults in the community, form relationships as they complete service projects, and often become inspired to pursue an area of interest as a vocation.

If these activities are not feasible, you might arrange for your child to shadow an adult friend at her or his workplace. Choose a day when you can bring your kids to each other's workplaces so they can begin to think about the jobs that appeal to them. Outdoor construction and landscaping may appeal to some, while indoor work like accounting or editing may appeal to others. By observing and interacting with adult role models, preteens begin to know themselves, identify their preferences, and develop respect for different kinds of people and the talents they bring to the world.

Tip 3. Form a support group.
Mothers and fathers who want to be effective parents need support from other like-minded people. Even if you begin with only one other parent, get started and form a supportive parent group. Try the suggestions in this book for building assets in your preteens. A lot of humorous situations develop in the preteen years, so enjoy yourselves and have fun!

REDUCE STRESS
TACKLE
FINANCES

part two:
Taking Care of Yourself

SEEK BALANCE
LOOK
FORWARD

TAKE TIME FOR YOURSELF

Putting your needs on the back burner until your preteen has what he or she needs is often just what parents do. Taking the burnt piece of chicken, drinking your coffee black when milk for morning cereal is low, postponing your own new coat purchase so your growing preteen can have one, and watching a Disney movie when what you really want to see is an adult chick-flick or action thriller—these are all examples many parents can relate to.

Putting children's needs first usually makes parents feel good. But when you stop feeling good and start feeling burdened or resentful, there's a problem. Minimizing care for yourself is not always good for kids. Children whose needs are always considered first cannot develop sensitivity to others' needs. It is much healthier for them to understand and respect that their parents' needs and feelings sometimes take precedence, too. Your kindness and consideration toward your preteen can model for him or her how to be as kind and considerate to others as you are.

Part Two is about taking care of yourself, because parents cannot give what they do not have themselves. When reserves of kindness, patience, humor, creativity, perspective, and compassion are depleted, your ability to parent well is diminished. Just when you need your sense of humor, you may not find anything funny in a certain situation. Just when your preteen has pushed your last button, you may find yourself out of ideas for responding creatively. To be an asset-building parent, it is important to feel in control and have resources to draw upon. Consider the following parenting tips for keeping your reserves well-stocked.

FIND SOURCES OF SUPPORT

Getting support from other parents is so important. They really do understand how you feel about your kids—the fear, frustration, joy, protectiveness, and hope—because they feel it, too. Sometimes raising preteens can seem overwhelming, especially when parents work so hard at doing it right. Having another parent to talk to or to vent feelings with can make a huge difference in your attitude and perspective. When problems seem too huge to handle, another parent may offer a suggestion that makes so much sense you wonder why you didn't think of it yourself.

Solutions are elusive when you become emotionally involved with a problem, because when you're upset, you think with the limbic, or emotional, part of your brain. Other parents, who really do understand what you are going through, can offer you objectivity and creativity, because they are not involved in the issue to the degree that you are.

↪ *Time for Yourself*

Tip 1. Form a support group with other parents.
Agree to meet at least monthly on a rotating basis—in group members' homes, at a coffee shop, or wherever it's convenient. The host can provide beverages and simple snacks. Agree on a topic beforehand, if helpful. You can use "Reflection and Discussion" statements throughout

Part One to focus on particular issues. Or open the discussion to a wide range of topics—bedtimes, curfews, clothing choices, cell phones, chores, discipline, and moodiness. Make sure everyone agrees to respect group members' privacy and keep conversations confidential—no gossiping.

Tip 2. Nurture your spiritual side.

Take time to refresh yourself spiritually by meditating, participating in a faith community, praying, walking in nature, or doing anything that makes you feel relaxed and refreshed. Develop or maintain a relationship with spiritual leaders and ask for help when necessary. Sometimes parents need a spiritual advisor to listen to their concerns and reassure them that they are doing the right things.

Tip 3. Seek counseling if you're depressed.

Untreated depression can lead to a variety of other issues, including physical problems and an inability to parent effectively. Sometimes people can become depressed without recognizing it. Tune in to your feelings. If you suspect you are depressed, seek counseling first by talking to your doctor, who can help you find a good counselor.

Tip 4. Enlist an advocate's help if your child is having academic or behavioral problems in school.

Talk to a guidance counselor, school psychologist, or local agency that offers parents support with school-related issues. Dealing with teachers and principals can be difficult for parents. Getting professional advice and enlisting an advocate can make an important difference in the situation.

Tip 5. Have fun!

Parents who balance work, parenting, extended family responsibilities, and household chores may find it difficult to take time out for themselves. You and your family will be much happier when you do. Choose activities that give you energy and revive your spirit: take a class, go swimming, play cards, meet friends for coffee, treat yourself to a sundae, browse in a bookstore, or go for a run. See a movie that you want to see without the kids. Think about what would make you happy, and do it. It may mean arranging childcare, but don't let that prevent you from taking time for yourself. You could work out an agreement with another parent to watch each other's kids so that you both can have a break. Try to do this at least twice a month, and encourage other parents to do the same.

CREATE A HEALTHY LIFESTYLE

Most parents are vigilant about making sure their kids have their shots, physical exams, and dental checkups. But often, parents don't do the same for themselves. Eventually preteens notice if you aren't practicing what you preach when it comes to diet, exercise, wellness visits, and sleep. If they see you don't eat a healthy diet, or get enough exercise and sleep, they'll feel justified in eating poorly and watching TV late into the evening. If you try to intervene, they may be likely to point to you and say, "Well, you do it." Don't get caught in that trap. The structure you create at home influences long-term behaviors that preteens develop. If you have a hard time doing things for yourself, remember that the self-care behaviors you model will have a long-lasting impact on your kids. Be healthy for them.

➤ *Time for Yourself*

Tip 1. Stock your refrigerator with fruits and vegetables for snacking.

Tip 2. Make and keep your yearly physical exam and dental appointments.
If money or health insurance is a problem, check out clinics that offer reduced rates.

Tip 3. Take a brisk 30-minute walk two to three times a week.

Tip 4. Turn off the TV at a reasonable hour, stop working or doing chores, and go to bed.
Take a book if you aren't yet sleepy. Health experts say many adults do not get enough sleep. Seven to nine hours of sleep is adequate for most adults.

Tip 5. If you feel lethargic, schedule a doctor's appointment to make sure nothing is physically wrong.

Tip 6. If you smoke, try to stop. Drink responsibly, if at all.
Excellent new medications are available to assist you in quitting. Avoid modeling any behavior that is unhealthy. Drink alcohol in moderation. You teach your preteen how to handle alcohol by your own example.

NURTURE YOUR RELATIONSHIP WITH YOUR PARTNER

If you share parenting responsibilities with a spouse or partner, one of the best gifts you can give your child is the model of a solid relationship with that person. Preteens learn more asset-building skills from seeing happy parents interact than from watching two harried people fight or fail to communicate. Kids need to see loving people enjoying one another, communicating with one another, and having fun together.

🔆 *Time for Yourself*

Tip 1. Make time alone for your partner and yourself each week.

Take turns doing the planning, and don't complain if you aren't thrilled by your partner's choices. Enjoy each other's company and keep an open mind. If your preteen is younger, hire a sitter and get out for a couple of hours. If that's not possible, order a pizza for the kids and cook a favorite dinner (or bring home take-out) for the two of you.

Tip 2. Surprise your partner or spouse with notes or other signs that communicate your love.

And compliment one another. It's too easy to become complacent and take each other for granted. Thank your partner for contributions and accomplishments that benefit the family, and acknowledge special talents: "You are so patient with the children." "Our kids have so much fun when you play with them."

LET GO OF GUILT

Guilt does no one any good, yet that doesn't mean parents aren't prone to feeling guilty at times. Not surprisingly, many parents second-guess their decisions at one time or another and wonder if they might have done things differently. Reflecting on past actions is actually a sign of intelligence and can lead to learning from mistakes and aiming to do better next time. That's not guilt—guilt is allowing yourself to feel that, through your actions or lack thereof, you have somehow disappointed others. Sometimes, others—including your preteen—may try to impose guilt on you, while at other times you impose it on yourself. Being consumed with guilt is unproductive for everyone.

Parents feel guilty about a wide range of situations. How about refusing to let your child socialize with another child you fear is a bad influence? Or not having money to buy your child the newest game system? Maybe it's not having a two-parent family because of separation, divorce, or death of a partner or spouse. Or not being able to give your child the time you would like because of work demands. Perhaps you feel guilty for saying hurtful things in an angry moment. The list can go on and on.

So how can you avoid falling into the guilt trap and become confident in your choices and parenting judgment? Try these ideas for dealing with guilt and becoming a more empowered, confident parent.

⟲ *Time for Yourself*

Tip 1. Stop using the word *should*. Stick to words that give choices and options.
Try saying might or could. "I'm thinking I *might* start to exercise." This is more effective than saying, "I *should* start to exercise," because you're not making a judgment you are considering an action.

Tip 2. Don't waste your energy feeling guilty for something over which you have no control.
And don't feel guilty if you can't give your preteens everything they want. Do the best you can with the resources you have, and give your child your time and attention as often as possible.

Tip 3. If you have done something to warrant feeling guilty, forgive yourself and move on.
Acknowledge your error, and vow to do better in the future.

Tip 4. Correct whatever it is that makes you feel guilty.
Make amends if necessary. For example, say to your preteen, "I realize that what I said was hurtful to you. I sometimes say things in anger that I shouldn't. I hope you can forgive me, and I'll try harder in the future to do better." By apologizing, you model a very important life skill for your child.

Tip 5. Give yourself a break.
Sometimes when you rest or focus on yourself for a little while, feelings of "I should be doing something productive" become all-consuming. Realize that taking care of yourself is a gift to the people you love, not just a gift to yourself. Allow yourself down time without guilt. Allow your partner the same consideration.

DEAL WITH STRESS

Parents of preteens inevitably cope with stress. And, like guilt, stress can be debilitating if it spins out of control. While a certain amount of stress is unavoidable, you can do certain things to let off steam when the pressure builds. Writing your stress triggers down on paper and devising plans to address them, can help make you feel more in control. Be sure to list what's going *right* in your family life to balance the perception that things are going poorly.

↻ *Time for Yourself*

Tip 1. Don't bottle up feelings.
Set aside time to talk regularly with your spouse or parenting partner about issues that bother you. Look for solutions to problems together.

Tip 2. Make time for exercise.
Walk the dog, weed the garden, go for a run, lift weights, mow the lawn, take a long bike ride, or go for a hike. Sustained exercise can lift your spirits and renew your energy, making you a better parent in the process.

Tip 3. Talk to friends.
Sometimes you just need a sympathetic listener to make you feel better. Use your friends as sounding boards, and then reciprocate, listening to them as well.

Tip 4. Identify what stresses you out about your kids, and make a plan to address it.
Is it their behavior? Lack of communication? Poor grades? Work with your child as a team to address what's going on. Hold a family meeting, and make a list of what needs to be done. Post the list where everyone can see it.

TACKLE FINANCES

Families often struggle financially as food, shelter, and clothing needs compete with other items in the family budget. In addition, preteens yearn for the latest in shoes, jeans, portable DVD and personal music players, videos, cell phones, computers, and game systems. The list often feels endless. Here are a few tips that can help ease financial pressures on everyone in the family.

⟲ *Time for Yourself*

Tip 1. Live within your means, and be sure your priorities are where you want them to be.

Your children will not die if they don't get all the material things they ask for, but they will suffer if you spend all your time earning money rather than parenting them. Given a choice, kids would rather have parents who laugh, work, play, and spend time with them rather than parents who substitute gifts for time.

Tip 2. Work within a budget.

Determine your monthly income and expenses. Create a manageable financial plan, and organize a system for paying bills on time. Keep envelopes together, try online bill paying, and set up a simple file system that helps you keep track of important papers. Seek financial counseling if you need help with finances.

Tip 3. Keep in mind that the preteen years are part of a self-centered developmental phase.

Preteens live in a material world that targets them with catchy marketing campaigns. While they lack the experience of working and earning their own money, they are often interested in finances, so this is a good time to introduce them to the "share, save, and spend" method of organizing their own money. Take time to help your preteen distinguish between wants and needs. If your family wants certain items, develop a savings plan with your children. Try not to stress yourself by going into debt for pleasure items (vacations, flat screen TVs, new cars). You are teaching monetary responsibility, which is a rarity in this era of credit card debt and consumerism.

Tip 4. Be honest with your children about your financial situation.

This doesn't mean you should tell them your bank balance. Rather, explain when their requests are beyond your means, without making them anxious. Describe where the family money must go first (mortgage, rent, utilities, food, clothing, transportation, insurance, and so on) before it can be spent on luxuries.

Tip 5. Give your kids your time instead of your checkbook.

Remember, when most people reflect on their preteen years, they recall times when their families ate favorite meals together or did simple things like roasting marshmallows in the fireplace or playing board games.

LOOK FORWARD

Parents who work hard to help their preteens build assets have the pleasure of watching them grow into self-sufficient young people who can carry on mature conversations, contribute to the effective running of the home, interact well socially, and achieve academically. It really is an exciting time to look forward to. While your parental role is gradually changing, don't worry, because throughout the preteen years you continue to be needed, just in a different way. Effective parents of preteens gracefully allow their children to assume more adult-like privileges without entirely letting go of them. So "let go" without letting go.

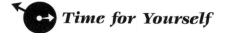 *Time for Yourself*

Tip 1. Be honest about your feelings with your preteen.

Tell your child you know he is growing up. Explain that while he believes he can do adult-like activities, you still need time to be sure. Then negotiate new rules that are appropriate for the activities he wants to do.

Tip 2. Change is ever-present when raising kids, and it seems the pace quickens as kids grow older.
You may feel that time is going by too fast. If that's the case, be sure to set aside time to spend with your preteen so that you can have some fun together and maintain your relationship. It also will enable you to observe and admire new capabilities, humor, and perspectives of the world.

Tip 3. Celebrate the new person you are helping to shape, who will one day take his or her place as a contributing member of society.
Mark special occasions in your preteen's life with celebratory dinners or outings that let her know how much you appreciate who she is today.

Tip 4. When preteens question rules or push the limits, they are doing just what preteens should be doing.
Try to keep that perspective when tempers flare and patience is limited. Preteens do not always accept redirection willingly, but know that you are aiming to support their best interests.

Tip 5. Allow yourself to feel your feelings.
It's natural to miss the young child who never questioned your authority and thought you were the wisest person on the planet. Parents sense when their kids begin moving away from them during the preteen years, and that can be scary and sad. Sometimes kids behave angrily at their parents so they can feel okay about separating from them. It hurts to be the target of their anger, but remember that separation has to happen for growth to continue. Kids often feel parents are the safest people in

the world to be angry at because they believe their parents will always love them—no matter what. Being a parent hurts sometimes, so cry when you need to, and laugh whenever you can!

BALANCE HOME AND WORK

Balancing the demands of both work and home can be exhausting and draining. Frazzled parents come home drained of energy because they have spent all of it at work, and kids, too, struggle with fluctuating emotions and new academic challenges. It's important for parents to figure out how to save energy for their most important investment—their kids.

Time for Yourself

Tip 1. Keep job responsibilities in perspective.
In a competitive world, you may feel the need to put in long hours. Your job is important. However, if working flexible hours is an option, try it in order to spend more time with your kids.

Tip 2. Prepare yourself mentally for entering your home after a long day at work.
Think positively about your kids, and communicate your happiness to be home with them again. Put the work issues on the back burner for the evening whenever possible.

Tip 3. Invite your preteens to take a walk after dinner or read in the same room with them while they do their homework.
Let them know that you value their company. Talk to them about things they are interested in. Being with your kids can reenergize you.

Tip 4. Avoid trying to be everything to everyone.

Share the load of responsibilities with your spouse, and your preteens, too. It is important for every family member to contribute in order to feel valued. Preteens can do chores that help alleviate household stress on parents (folding laundry, walking dogs and feeding animals, emptying trash, watering plants, helping cook, cleaning the kitchen, and so on).

PLAN FOR THE FUTURE

For most parents, it's inevitable that children will one day leave home. That time may still seem far off, but know that once it arrives, parents often feel at a loss, if only temporarily. Embrace the notion that you will have accomplished an amazing task when they do leave home. You will have given your children the Developmental Assets to follow their dreams. However, make sure you're ready for that day by developing interests and plans for your future.

It may be hard to envision that time now as you make your way through the preteen and early adolescent years, but it will arrive sooner than you think. Maintaining or developing your own interests is as important now as it is for the years to come. Preteens benefit from having interesting, inquisitive parents who are invested in their own learning and in doing fulfilling things.

Time for Yourself

Tip 1. Seek activities that you and your spouse or partner enjoy together.

Golfing, dancing, socializing with friends, reading and discussing books, cooking together, walking together—try whatever draws you toward each other!

Tip 2. You do have time to live many of your dreams after your children leave home.
And your experiences as a parent can make you a valuable, wiser employee with much to contribute in the workplace.

Tip 3. If you've put some plans on hold, shake off the dust and see if they are still important to you.
Whether it's going back to school or landing a dream job, do the research now to see what you need to do to achieve those dreams.

Tip 4. Avoid attaching your dreams to your children's accomplishments, now or later.
Don't depend on your children to create your social activities. Your children will one day want to live their own lives. Aim to share in their lives, not depend on them.

Tip 5. To be an interesting person, it's essential to develop your own interests.
Volunteer in the community; offer your ideas, time, and support for projects that matter to you; and seek ways to find purpose in life.

Tip 6. Remember that you'll never stop being a parent.
The unsettled feelings you may experience when children move from one phase to the next will ease as you realize you are still a parent to your kids, no matter how old they are. Your role will evolve, just as it did when you moved from parenting preschoolers to parenting pre-teens. Enjoy the ride and all of its twists and turns!

part three:

Taking Care of Your Preteen

FOCUS ON YOUR PRETEEN

Butterflies begin as humble caterpillars. As they wait patiently in their chrysalises, nature takes its course. When the time is right, they struggle to break free from the safety of the chrysalis. Squeezing through the tight casing removes the sticky residue from their wings, allowing butterflies to take flight and become the beautiful creatures that they are.

Comparing the transformational struggle of butterflies to preteens' developmental experiences makes sense. The preteens before you today are really adults in the making. The struggles they face and the challenges they present to you now are part of a necessary and exciting process. When preteens start to outgrow the safe cocoon parents have created for them, they are doing exactly what they need to do to reach adulthood. They must stretch themselves and expand their horizons, sometimes trying to be more adult-like than they are prepared to be. At other times, they may become stuck in the cocoon and need encouragement to move forward. As an asset-building parent, your appropriate response to these struggles is critical to your preteens' success.

Part Three focuses on issues prevalent in preteens' lives and offers some strategies for responding in asset-building ways to your preteens' needs. Issues are addressed in alphabetical order for easy reference.

AFTER-SCHOOL HOURS

ASSET 11: Family Boundaries
ASSET 17: Creative Activities
ASSET 18: Child Programs

For the most part, kids' school hours and parents' business hours are out of sync. School days may start after a parent's work day begins, and they end at least two to three hours before most parents leave work. As kids become preteens, before- and after-school childcare becomes less widely available. When preteens reach the age of 11 or 12, parents begin to leave them unsupervised more often. Preteens who go home alone after school often face a good amount of unsupervised free time. The U.S. Census Bureau estimated in 2002 that there are about 6.1 million latchkey kids. And according to the National Safe Kids Campaign, 4.5 million children are injured each year, most of them kids who are unsupervised after school (Safe Kids Worldwide, www.safekids.org).

Many parents are relieved when they can finally let their preteens go home after school. After-school care is one less arrangement to make and one less bill to pay. There is something comforting about thinking that the kids are home where they can grab a snack and get started on homework. Many parents feel safer if their children call to check in with them when they arrive home. However, this can create a false sense of security for many reasons.

Parents may think children are responsible and capable simply because they are growing older. Some preteens have started babysitting, and parents often believe preteens can make good decisions for themselves since they can be paid to watch other kids. Neither of these assumptions may be safe to make. The after-school hours are fraught with temptations for preteens, ranging from eating too much before dinner to having friends over without getting parents' permission first.

Law enforcement experts assert that during after-school hours, many unsupervised kids experiment with alcohol, other drugs, and sexual situations, and are more likely to be involved in a crime. Even if your preteens aren't experimenting with risk-taking behavior, it is important to know exactly how they're spending those hours before you arrive home.

❗ *Parenting Tips*

- *Structure your child's time as much as possible in your absence.* Limit time spent in front of the TV. Sitting on a couch watching TV is an attractive option to many preteens, but one that often interferes with getting homework done, being physically active, or being creative.

- *Encourage some physical exercise,* whether it's working out to an exercise DVD, jumping rope, walking with a trusted friend, or dancing to music.

- *Stock up on healthy, appealing snacks.* Most kids come home from school hungry for a snack. Leave a note suggesting foods and drinks your child can have. Discourage over-snacking.

- *Develop a daily schedule or routine for your child to follow* (have a snack, do homework or chores, and only then watch a limited amount of TV or play video games). Review homework so that your child knows you expect it to be done, or at least started, by the time you get home.

- *Teach your child ways to remain safe* (never open the door to a stranger, don't admit being home alone to a caller, leave emergency telephone numbers in sight for fire, police, ambulance, and parents).

- *Be clear about your expectations regarding having friends over when you are not present.*

- *Install filters or blocks on home computers* to ensure that your child cannot get or receive information from Web sites you think are inappropriate.

- *If your school, YMCA, religious community, or city recreation center offers after-school programs, consider sending your preteen.* Some schools provide later activity buses that drop kids off after school clubs and intramural sports teams have met. Many community programs offer opportunities for socialization, physical exercise, creative projects, and safe places for kids to interact and develop interests. They may also provide tutoring programs for kids who need extra help with schoolwork.

ALCOHOL, TOBACCO, AND OTHER DRUGS

ASSET 11: Family Boundaries
ASSET 13: Neighborhood Boundaries
ASSET 31: Healthy Lifestyle
ASSET 35: Resistance Skills

Parents often believe their children are not the ones using alcohol, tobacco, or other drugs, thinking the statistics they've heard cannot possibly apply to their own kids. But sometimes when reality sinks in, it's too late. There are serious consequences when preteens begin smoking or using controlled or illegal substances. Of all addictive behaviors, cigarette smoking is the one most likely to be established during adolescence. The younger preteens start smoking, the more likely they will become addicted to nicotine. Tobacco users are at much greater risk for using other substances, as well.

For some preteens, alcohol use starts in middle school. The University of Michigan's 2006 *Monitoring the Future* survey revealed that 20 percent of 8th graders reported being drunk one or more times, and 34 percent drank alcohol before the age of 13 (www.monitoringthefuture.org). Marijuana ranks highly, too, as a preteen drug of choice. In some areas of the country, inhalants (aerosols, gasoline, paint, correction fluid, permanent markers, and others) are a favorite of middle school-aged kids, due to their dizzying effects and easy availability. Younger children, who may not have easy access to alcohol, also experiment with over-the-counter (OTC) drugs, such as cough medicine.

Preteens watch what others do and often imitate those behaviors. They can't wait to "try on" adult roles, and for a multitude of reasons, drinking is one behavior that is very attractive to them. They like the taste of sweet alcoholic drinks and their relaxing, disinhibiting effects. When preteens cannot get the alcohol that they perceive to be so desirable, they sometimes settle for

Psychologist David Walsh, Ph.D., author of *WHY Do They Act That Way?* notes, "The earlier a youngster starts to drink, the higher the probability that he or she will have alcohol problems or alcoholism as an adult. This correlation probably occurs because drinking while the brain is developing encourages the brain to decide, through the firing and wiring process, that it needs alcohol. Adults would have to drink more heavily to be as likely to wire a tendency for alcohol use into their mature brains. . . . Adolescents are much more likely than adults to get addicted to nicotine, the most prominent and powerful chemical in tobacco, and they get addicted much more quickly" (Walsh, 2004).

more easily accessible drugs, such as inhalants, cough medicine, and over-the-counter drugs or pills they find in the family medicine cabinet. Unless preteens have clear guidance from their parents, and are connected with a positive peer group, they may not perceive substance use as negative. Many believe that prescription or OTC drugs are not harmful since they are legal.

If preteens often see parents or older siblings drinking, smoking, or taking prescription drugs inappropriately, they may consider the behavior normal. As kids are reaching puberty at an increasingly younger age, they are attracted earlier to adult-like activities, including substance use. Fitting in and being "cool" is an important factor in preteens' minds and in making decisions. If using illegal substances is the pathway to acceptance, some preteens will take that path. Of course, their brains are not yet fully capable of anticipating the consequences of their behavior. To them, the immediate reward of acceptance outweighs potential negative consequences.

In addition to their inherent need to fit in, preteens are subjected to overpowering media messages—frequent depictions of alcohol, tobacco, and other drug use in TV and popular movies; the substance-fueled behaviors of teen icons; and alcohol or drug references in popular music. However, Columbia University's National Center on Addiction and Substance Abuse 2001 teen survey of 1,000 12- to 17-year-old teens indicated that parental disapproval was the primary reason youth chose not to use alcohol, tobacco, and other drugs. Those students said they knew their parents would disapprove of such behavior. Clearly, parents have immense power to influence their children's choices if they take the necessary steps to do so. Use your influence while you have it (www.casacolumbia.org).

Spotlight on Boundaries-and-Expectations Assets

Parents who model restraint in the use of alcohol and do not use tobacco have children who are more likely to do the same. Your attitudes toward alcohol and tobacco are taught early to your children by what you say and do. It's critical to model appropriate use of alcohol and to discuss your expectations with your children regarding alcohol or tobacco use long before you think they'll want to try a cigarette or take a drink.

❗ *Parenting Tips*

- *Be explicit about your values.* Openly discuss your feelings about alcohol, tobacco, and other drug use during meals with your children or in casual conversation when children will be sure to hear you (in the car or on the phone). Kids often listen better when they overhear what you're saying, rather than getting a lecture.

- *Make it clear that you expect your child not to use alcohol until she is of legal drinking age, and not to use tobacco at all.* Usually, most children try to meet their parents' expectations. Your preteens do care what you think, especially if you have established solid relationships built on trust and love.

- *Be aware of what your child's friends say and do.* Peer behavior is a prime influence for preteens, and what friends do is a strong predictor of what your child will do.

- *Chaperone preteen parties.* Occasionally enter the room unannounced. Call parents to make sure chaperones are going to be at parties that your child attends and invite them to help at yours. Share your knowledge and concerns about alcohol and other drug use.

- *Monitor the legal drinks your child consumes.* Preteens often drink high-sugar, high-caffeine energy drinks in excess, thinking them harmless. However, caffeine and sugar, as well as energy drinks containing certain herbs, can have an impact on your child's health and behavior. Kids who try to change the way they feel by consuming such drinks undermine, rather than enhance, their abilities. Set them straight with your own modeling and discussion of nutritional facts.

- *Be aware that OTC drugs are popular with preteens.* They routinely abuse cough medicine and cold remedies containing dextromethorphan. Preteens can purchase these remedies at most drug stores (although some stores now keep certain cold remedies behind the counter to discourage abuse).

ATTENTION DISORDERS

ASSET 6: Parent Involvement in Schooling
ASSET 12: School Boundaries
ASSET 22: Learning Engagement
ASSET 38: Self-Esteem

According to the National Institutes of Health, attention deficit disorder (AD/HD), with or without hyperactivity, is the most frequently diagnosed behavior disorder of childhood, and affects approximately three to five percent of school-aged children, with boys diagnosed more often than girls. Attention deficit/hyperactivity disorder symptoms include inattentiveness, overactivity, impulsivity, or a combination of all three. In order for these behaviors to be diagnosed as AD/HD, the frequency and degree of symptoms must be out of the normal range for the child's age and developmental stage.

New neuroscience research shows that the brains of children diagnosed with AD/HD differ from other children's. In addition, AD/HD is often inherited. However, AD/HD is easily confused with other disorders, including depression, anxiety, learning disabilities, tic disorders, and behavior problems. To obtain an accurate diagnosis of AD/HD, parents must consult qualified professionals who will consider a wide variety of relevant factors (including behavior issues, depression, anxiety, family dissolution, and allergies) (National Library of Medicine, www.nlm.nih.gov).

Psychologist Thomas Armstrong, Ph.D., doubts AD/HD is as prevalent as it appears. He believes contemporary culture has produced a generation of media-fed youngsters with short attention spans. He asserts that AD/HD has become a convenient diagnosis for some to explain away symptoms that could, in fact, be related to other issues (family dissolution, food allergies, boredom, or teaching styles, among others) that are incompatible with a child's learning style (thomasarmstrong.com). Many sources of help are available for parents whose children may have AD/HD. For more information and support, link to the Web site of Children and Adults with Attention Deficit/Hyperactivity Disorder (CHADD) at www.chadd.org.

Children diagnosed with AD/HD may be prescribed medication to help control symptoms. Newer medications, in addition to Ritalin™, are now available. Medication, which a medical doctor must prescribe, can be very effective for those who are accurately diagnosed as having AD/HD. Some doctors recommend that medications be taken all year, not just when a child is in school. This is because AD/HD is a chronic condition

Symptoms of AD/HD

- Failing to pay close attention to details
- Making careless mistakes
- Not listening when being spoken to directly
- Not following through on instructions and failing to finish schoolwork and chores
- Experiencing difficulty organizing tasks and activities
- Losing personal items, assignments, pencils, books, or tools needed for tasks
- Being easily distracted
- Becoming forgetful in daily activities
- Fidgeting with feet or hands or squirming in seat
- Running around or climbing in inappropriate settings
- Finding it difficult to play quietly
- Talking excessively and moving constantly
- Blurting out answers before questions have been completed
- Experiencing difficulty waiting for a turn
- Interrupting or intruding on others during games or conversations (www.nlm.nih.gov)

that affects social interactions and organizational skills, as well as school performance. Young people who are developing social and relational skills need help managing their symptoms to successfully interact with peers and develop skills they will need as adults. Proper medication can enable kids who have AD/HD to develop the social and organizational skills that allow them to experience positive social relationships.

Raising a preteen who has AD/HD can be confusing, frustrating, and lonely for parents. Remember that you are not alone and that your child is not being willfully troublesome. Often kids are just as frustrated and confused by their symptoms as are parents, teachers, and friends. Be resilient and recognize that your preteen has talents and resources that others may not have. Help your child to see that having AD/HD is a condition that he or she can learn to manage successfully.

! Parenting Tips

- *Get an accurate diagnosis.* Do not accept the diagnosis until qualified professionals meet, observe, interview, and test your child. If your intuition tells you that something other than AD/HD is going on, consider obtaining a second or third opinion.

- *Provide structure, checklists, quiet places for homework, and strategies for your preteen to develop skills to resist impulsivity.* Your parental support is critical to helping your preteen manage AD/HD during this period of rapid development.

- *Make sure your preteen takes any necessary medication consistently.*

AUDITORY PROCESSING

ASSET 6: Parent Involvement in Schooling
ASSET 12: School Boundaries
ASSET 22: Learning Engagement
ASSET 38: Self-Esteem

One of the most common areas for learning difficulties in preteens is in auditory processing—the taking in and putting out of information. Experts don't know the exact cause of auditory processing problems, but have identified some likely factors. Children who have experienced head trauma, lead poisoning, or multiple ear infections as infants may later experience interrupted language development. When they are supposed to develop speech and language connections in the brain (making sense of sounds, words, and tones), such children may not hear clearly and store the information for future use.

To discriminate between sounds like car and bar, for example, babies must hear clearly. An interruption in language development often surfaces later when a child has difficulty with reading, verbal expression, written expression, following instructions, sequencing, or participating in conversations.

Auditory processing disorders are sometimes confused with Attention Deficit/Hyperactivity Disorder (AD/HD) because of the appearance of inattention. Children may have multiple, undiagnosed auditory processing problems. Even though they may seem to hear and speak normally, children may have residual learning problems that affect school success. It is critical that parents and teachers address auditory processing issues to prevent a child from becoming discouraged with learning. Specific clinical tests are used by psychologists, speech-language pathologists, and audiologists to diagnose auditory processing problems, including the Clinical Evaluation of Language Fundamentals (CELF-3) and the Test of Language Development (TOLD). The good news is that, with appropriate therapeutic intervention, many children can successfully address their auditory processing problems.

❗ *Parenting Tips*

- *If you suspect an auditory processing problem in your preteen,* share your concerns about your

Checklist for Auditory Processing Disorders

Reflect on your child's current and earlier behaviors as you read through the checklist.

- Is your child easily distracted or unusually bothered by loud or sudden noises?

- Are noisy environments upsetting to your child?

- Does your child's behavior and performance improve in quieter settings?

- Does your child have difficulty following directions, whether simple or complicated?

- Does your child have reading, writing, spelling, or other speech-language difficulties?

- Is abstract information difficult for your child to comprehend?

- Are verbal math problems difficult for your child?

- Is your child disorganized and forgetful?

- Are conversations hard for your child to follow?
  (www.kidshealth.org)

child's apparent learning difficulties with your family doctor or pediatrician. A complete physical exam can help rule out other undiagnosed health problems in your preteen.

- *Educate yourself*—visit the Web site of the National Institute on Deafness and Other Communication Disorders at www.nidcd.nih.gov for specific guidelines on auditory processing disorder in children.

- *Be patient;* it often takes more time than parents think to diagnose the source of a child's learning issues. Seek support from teachers, school counselors, and other parents who have had similar experiences.

BULLYING

ASSET 2: Positive Family Communication
ASSET 5: Caring School Climate
ASSET 10: Safety
ASSET 28: Integrity
ASSET 30: Responsibility
ASSET 37: Personal Power

Bullying has plagued kids for generations. A 2004 Kids Health KidsPoll survey of more than 1,200 9- to 13-year-old boys and girls revealed the following:

- *86 percent* said they've seen someone else being bullied.

- *48 percent* said they've been bullied.

- *42 percent* admitted to bullying other kids at least once in a while (www.kidshealth.org).

Victims of bullying are not the only kids damaged. Bystanders also are affected by bullying because they often are afraid to associate with the victim, fear reporting incidents to adults, experience feelings of sadness for not standing up for another, are drawn into bullying through peer pressure, or may feel unsafe or out of control.

Recent school shootings and many youth suicides are a tragic culmination of the effects of bullying. Victims often turn violence toward themselves or their perpetrators. Other long-term consequences of bullying include negative effects on adolescent and adult relationships and increased risk of substance abuse and depression. Parents are often the last to know about bullying situations because victims are too ashamed or afraid to tell anyone.

Kids experience conflict as a part of growing up. There is, however, a big difference between normal conflict and bullying. On its Web site, the Committee for Children describes the differences between normal conflict and bullying. Normal conflict generally entails disagreements or misunderstandings, students who are matched in strength and status, a lack of conflict resolution skills, or a lack of anger management skills. Bullying, on the other hand, entails repeated negative actions against a person, an imbalance of power or status between bully and victim, intent to harm, and sometimes physical, emotional, and sexual aggression; gossip and insults; and exclusion from a group or activities (www.cfchildren.org).

It is important to note that boys and girls bully differently. Boys are more apt to bully in a physical way, while girls tend to engage in "relational aggression." This means that girls may bully through ostracism, gossip, hurtful verbal abuse, and manipulation (Wiseman, 2002).

If Your Child Is Being Bullied

Kids who are bullied rarely ask adults for help for fear of making the situation worse. They believe that getting their perpetrator in trouble will increase the bullying. For the most part, they are correct. Bullies are extremely good at hiding their actions from adults, especially on the playground, the Internet, in the locker room, or even in the classroom. Teachers and adults often perceive them as friendly and popular. Their victims are usually quiet, unassertive, less popular, and, therefore, less powerful. It is critical that parents and adults in the school be attuned to signs that a child is being bullied.

Cyberbullying is a form of bullying on the Internet that includes posting gossip, saying mean things, harassing with nasty messages, and using e-mail, instant messaging, and Web postings to hurt feelings or take revenge. This activity can be devastating to the victim. Cyber bullies feel empowered because they are safely ensconced behind anonymous computer screens. The speed of the Internet and the anonymity of writers make this an especially effective way to bully.

Signs of Being Bullied

- Inventing illness to avoid school (stomachache, headache, etc.)
- Lost belongings or missing money
- Sleeping problems
- Bedwetting
- Irritability
- Poor concentration
- Unexpected changes in routine
- Problems with schoolwork (www.kidshealth.org)

❗ *Parenting Tips*

- *If you suspect your preteen is being bullied, do some investigation.* Ask your child questions that will give you clues: "What is it like on the bus?" "Who do you eat lunch with?" "What's happening in gym class?" Consult your preteen's teachers. Ask pointed questions.

- *Listen to your child.* If he or she tells you about being bullied, don't become angry—that will only make it worse.

- *Acknowledge your child's feelings.* Provide assurance that you will take action and that your child is not to blame. Explain that bullies have their own problems and take them out unfairly on innocent people.

- *If your child is being bullied on the Internet, alert police since this is a serious offense.*

- *If the bullying happens in school, consult with your child's counselor, teacher, or principal and explain the situation.* Give as many details of who, where, and when the bullying takes place so that teachers can be in the right place to catch the bully in action. To help your child avoid being the target of retaliation, insist that teachers not tell the bully you informed them about the problem.

- *Because bullies and victims are not on equal footing, it is not helpful to tell your preteen, "You just have to stand up for yourself. Don't let them scare you" or "The next time that happens, just tell the teacher."* This advice alone doesn't empower a child to solve the problem on his own when he is ill-equipped to change the power imbalance. Bullying is an adult problem that can usually only be resolved with adult intervention.

- *Most schools experience some form of bullying among students.* Find out if your child's school has a no-bullying policy. Offer information to your school about anti-bullying programs if the administration is unaware that a problem exists (see "Online Resources" on page 173).

- *If your preteen is quiet by temperament, make sure she has social activities to enjoy and feel good about.* If your child is shy, help her identify kids to socialize with, and invite them over. It is critical for your preteen to have a social network. Having even just a couple of friends makes your child less a target for bullies.

If Your Child Is the Bully

Parents are sometimes shocked to learn that their own children are doing the bullying. Kids bully others for a variety of reasons. They may not consider what they are doing to be wrong or hurtful. Their need to show off and be popular may outweigh any consideration they have for another's feelings. They may be angry or insecure. They also may have been bullied and resorted to bullying behavior to avoid being bullied again. Some young people, unfortunately, have been exposed to bullying in the home and see it as normal behavior. Whatever the reason, intervene with bullying behavior as soon as possible.

According to clinical child psychologist Michelle New, Ph.D., of Gaithersburg, Maryland, "Bullies are at risk for problems, too. Bullying is violence, and it often leads to more violent behavior as the bully grows up. It's estimated that one out of four elementary-school bullies will have a criminal record by the time they are 30. Some teen bullies end up being rejected by their peers and lose friendships as they grow older. Bullies may also fail in school and not have the career or relationship success that other people enjoy" (www.kidshealth.org).

❗ *Parenting Tips*

- *Calmly tell your child you are disappointed in his behavior, and assure him that you love him but despise the bullying he is doing.*

- *Ask why the bullying behavior is occurring and whether he has been bullied by others.*

- *If your child won't talk to you, consult a counselor or psychologist.* Get help for your child.

- *Teach and model respectful treatment of all people, regardless of their differences.*

- *In conversation, speculate how other people might feel in specific situations to develop empathy and respect for others' feelings.*

- *Observe your child's social interactions and praise appropriate behavior.*

- *Stop any show of aggression (verbal, physical, emotional) immediately and discuss different ways to behave.*

Bullies can learn different and healthier ways of interacting with parents' help. Work with your preteen to discover what he may lack in his life that leads to bullying behavior (poor self-esteem, learning struggles, poor peer role models, jealousy, anger, insensitivity to others' feelings, feeling neglected by parents, and so on). It takes time and energy to stop bullying behavior, but it is critical to help a child overcome this ultimately self-defeating behavior.

CHAPERONES AND SHOPPING MALLS

ASSET 10: Safety
ASSET 11: Family Boundaries
ASSET 14: Adult Role Models

Chaperones accompany young people on activities to supervise and ensure their safety and good judgment. One of the most common venues many parents consider safe for unaccompanied preteens is the shopping mall. However, malls also are great places for preteens to get into trouble. Preteens who are not chaperoned may take the opportunity to experiment with flirting or other sexual behaviors or copy negative behaviors (swearing, rudeness, and consuming drinks loaded with sugar, caffeine, and energy boosters). Preteens can become easy victims of crime. Preteen girls, who often appear older than their years, may appeal to older kids and adults who are interested in connecting with them.

Unsupervised groups of young people have prompted various shopping malls to ban youth under 18 after a certain time unless they are chaperoned. But, until you are convinced that your children have the maturity and common sense to make consistently good decisions and resist negative peer pressure, use chaperones regardless of the activity.

❗ *Parenting Tips*

- *Know where your preteens are going and with whom at all times.* Check to see if they have given you accurate information. Call another parent to introduce yourself if your children will be at their home. Offer to send food and invite the parent to call you at any time to discuss activities the kids are doing together.

- *Make yourself available to drive preteens to movies, malls, restaurants, skating rinks, or arcades.* Make sure the kids know that you will be in the area, and tell them when and where to meet you later. Be nearby so that you notice if some kids are not where they are supposed to be.

- *Communicate clear expectations to all the kids under your supervision.* If you see anyone acting inappropriately, intervene immediately. Sometimes preteens test adults, thinking you will not confront them. Send a firm message that you mean what you say.

- *If your community doesn't offer safe, supervised places for preteens to socialize, join other parents and community members to work with youth to develop a teen center.*

CHOKING GAME

ASSET 31: Healthy Lifestyle
ASSET 35: Resistance Skills

The choking game is an old, unwelcome practice that involves squeezing the neck or chest until the person being squeezed nearly loses consciousness or passes out. The idea is to temporarily deprive the brain of oxygen in order to experience the "high" of oxygenated blood rushing back to the brain when pressure is released. Many preteens devise ways to do this alone, using belts or other devices that squeeze the neck. Other names for this game are airplaning, the black-out or pass out game, gasp, funky chicken, and space monkey, among others.

Unfortunately, young people have died in the midst of this activity because they lost consciousness before they could release the ligature. Preteens don't consider this activity dangerous because it does not involve alcohol or other drugs. They may enjoy the euphoric and dizzying effects caused by oxygen deprivation and the subsequent rush of blood to the brain. Preteens who play this game are also attracted to the entertainment of watching their peers lose consciousness and behave erratically. Kids this age simply don't always consider the serious consequences of such behavior.

This activity pops up sporadically and spreads among kids by word of mouth. Many preteens are aware of the game, even if they do not play it. Tragically, parents of children who have died from playing the game often aren't aware of the game. In one case, the parents had noticed marks on their son's neck, but when asked about the marks, were told by their son that the family cat had scratched him. The parents later learned their son had been playing the game alone for weeks, repeatedly tightening a belt around his neck. They accepted their son's explanation for the marks and didn't investigate further, never suspecting their son was engaging in this dangerous activity. After their child's death, they wanted all parents to be aware of this potentially fatal game (see "Online Resources" on page 173).

Signs of the Choking Game

- Inexplicable bruises or red marks around the neck
- Ligatures (bed sheets, belts, tee shirts, ties, ropes) tied in strange knots or found in unusual places
- Frequent severe headaches
- Wear marks on furniture (bunk beds, closet rods) from previous incidents
- Disorientation or grogginess after being alone
- Unusual need for privacy (locked bedroom doors)
- Bloodshot eyes, pinpoint bruising around the eyes
- Changes in attitude (aggressive behavior) or different friends

! Parenting Tips

- *Talk to your preteens about the dangers of the choking game.* It's important that they understand the truth from you before hearing about the game from someone else. Ensure that they know the game causes the death of brain cells from passing out and that accidental death or brain damage can result.

- *Help preteens devise strategies to resist peer pressure to engage in this activity.*

- *Remove items that could be used as ligatures if you suspect your child might try this.*

- *Alert other parents and school personnel if you find out that anyone is doing this.* (dylan-the-boy-blake.com)

CLOTHES AND HAIR

ASSET 11: Family Boundaries
ASSET 12: School Boundaries
ASSET 32: Planning and Decision Making

Kids of this age begin noticing designer labels and start to show interest in wearing the "right" styles. You might be surprised to hear your child say that a perfectly good pair of jeans or shoes just won't work. Preteens can be tough critics of themselves and each other, and may face harsh scrutiny by their peers. It doesn't help that kids' style choices are shaped by retail buyers who promote preteen fashions that are more suitable for young adults.

Finding shirts and jeans that keep the four Bs covered (bellies, buns, breasts, and backs) can be a challenge. Preteens may become less sure of their changing bodies and are confused by society's encouragement to dress in overly sophisticated, provocative ways. Girls in particular may perceive themselves as being more capable than they really are of handling sexual issues when they dress like adult women. Help your preteen feel good about her developing body by shopping with her for clothes that you can both live with. It may mean several trips to the mall, or time devoted to looking at clothing catalogs online together, but the more time you spend matching appropriate styles to their age and maturity level, the happier you and your preteen will be.

As for hairstyles, every generation has its signature looks. Preteens have always established their own styles to separate themselves from parents and other adults. It's just what kids do. And the best part about hair is that it always grows out.

❗ *Parenting Tips*

- *Understand and acknowledge the pressure that your child may feel to fit in with peers.*

- *Compromise when you can to accommodate your child's taste in clothes, but avoid overruling your values when it comes to expense or fit.*

- *Don't buy clothes for your preteen that are sexually suggestive or are printed with messages that mention alcohol, other drug use, and risky behaviors.*

- *Help your child understand that clothes convey particular messages, and certain occasions dictate dressier attire (for example, school, recitals, and religious services).* Teach your child what's appropriate to wear in a variety of settings.

- *When you and your child go clothes shopping, share responsibility for sticking to a budget.* It is important that preteens learn to make wise choices and care for their clothes. Encourage your kids to save money and wait until they have enough to afford more expensive purchases. Being able to postpone gratification is both an asset and a sign of emotional intelligence.

- *Follow your school's dress code for clothes and hairstyles.* Intervene when your preteen's style becomes an issue at school. Help your child understand the reasons for the rules.

- *Encourage your child to wash her hair regularly and offer an incentive by letting her choose her own shampoo and conditioner.* Give her the privacy she needs to shower and bathe.

- *When it comes to hairstyles, instead of complaining, try to remember that your preteen is trying out a new persona.* Acknowledge your child's hairstyle without being judgmental. For example, "Your haircut sure shows off your beautiful eyes." or "I like your hair style. Do think about how you want to keep it up as it grows out."

- *Pick your battles wisely.* You may dislike your preteen's hairstyle or color but, luckily, hair grows out and styles do change. In the grand scheme of things, hair is pretty insignificant.

COMPUTERS AND TECHNOLOGY

ASSET 10: Safety
ASSET 11: Family Boundaries

Computers, cell phones, personal music and DVD players, hand-held games, and electronic organizers are a part of most kids' lives these days. These are remarkable instruments, and can be wonderful tools when used appropriately. Advances in technology make support, information, and instant connections available in seconds.

But technology also has its downsides. In addition to the irritations of spam, computer viruses, and pop-up advertising, preteen computer users also have to deal with sheer electronic overload. Kids in particular can easily become distracted from schoolwork by video and computer games, may be tempted to use technology to cheat on tests and projects, and are sometimes bullied by other students via texting and instant-messaging (IMing).

It is unfortunately true that unscrupulous adults do occasionally victimize kids through the Internet.

One of the ironies of technology is that kids are quick to assimilate and use it, far more quickly than many parents. Adults often aren't familiar with the Web sites preteens visit, what chat rooms they frequent, or how to fully use available technological features. Do stay informed about uses of the technology you allow your child to access and provide structure and boundaries that will keep your child safe.

❗ *Parenting Tips*

- *Set a limit on the amount of time your child spends on video games and the computer.* Using the Internet for school research projects, e-mail, and a limited amount of game-playing is appropriate, but it's often easy for preteens to neglect physical exercise or face-to-face interactions with friends.

- Kids use the Internet for social networking far more than many parents realize. *Discourage preteens from placing a personal page on social networking sites such as MySpace.* For more information about Web sites like MySpace, Facebook, and YouTube, see www.wiredsafety.org.

- *Keep computers in a common area like a den, kitchen corner, or home office so that you can monitor the sites your kids are visiting.*

- *Know who your preteen is IMing and ask what they like to talk about.* Learn the vocabulary of instant messaging. For example, *lol* is "laugh out loud" and *pir* is "parent in room." You can find other acronyms under "Fun With AIM" at www.aim.com.

- *Be respectful of your children's school environment*—insist that preteens leave Game Boys, cell phones, iPods, and other technology at home so that they don't become a distraction (or target for theft).

- *Don't purchase a Web cam for your preteen unless you are able to closely monitor its use.* The dangers of having one outweigh the fun it may offer.

- *Many local police departments designate an Internet expert who speaks to parent organizations and other community groups, helping parents stay on top of technology issues that impact the safety of their children.* They can provide information on setting up Web site blocks, filters, and other controls.

- *Talk with your preteen about "stranger danger" on the Internet.* Tell him not to give out personal information, phone numbers, school name, friends' names, or home address. Make sure your child knows never to meet someone he has met on the Internet. If your child insists on a meeting with a new Internet friend, chaperone and insist on being able to communicate with the new friend's parents.

- *Monitor the video games your kids play.* Some popular games are exceptionally violent or sexual, and game ratings don't always tell the full story. Many media experts believe that repeated exposure to the visual stimulation of video games alters the preteen brain, which is being molded by direct experience (Walsh, 2004).

CONFLICT RESOLUTION

ASSET 10: Safety
ASSET 33: Interpersonal Competence
ASSET 36: Peaceful Conflict Resolution

Conflict is an inevitable and normal part of preteens' lives. Characteristics of normal conflict vary with age and developmental level, and may include teasing, arguing, concerns related to issues of fairness, and sometimes verbal or physical fights. Preteens can learn how to resolve conflict peacefully and effectively by observing parents and other adults modeling appropriate conflict resolution (see "Online Resources" on page 173). Peaceful conflict resolution is critical to life success. Some schools offer programs that teach conflict resolution skills to students, but the best teachers are often parents.

Parents can talk about and demonstrate the difference between being assertive and aggressive. Assertive behavior flows from self-confidence and a belief in one's right to fair treatment. Assertive people know how to meet their needs without trying to control or hurt anyone else. They are sensitive to others' needs while protecting their own interests. Aggressive behavior flows from anger and a belief that others are "out to get you." Aggressive people view themselves as victims of other people or circumstances over which they have no control. They use intimidation or bullying to get their needs met. Over the long term, assertive people are more successful in meeting their own needs. If you can show your preteen the difference, you will be modeling valuable negotiation skills for life.

Parenting Tips

- *Make sure your preteen understands the difference between bullying and normal conflict.* When he experiences a conflict, help him look at both sides of an issue.

- *Teach her to wait until everyone is calmer to address a conflict.* Explain that the brain cannot think clearly when a person is upset.

- *Help him identify a few ideas for compromise before talking to the other person to resolve a conflict.*

- *Demonstrate the use of "I" statements rather than "you" statements* (for example, "I'm feeling really frustrated because I asked you last week to repay the money I lent you, and you haven't done it yet"). Place emphasis on expressing feelings appropriately.

- *Show preteens how to be firm about what they want without being threatening* (for example, "I have to have my money no later than Friday so that I can pay my mom back. If not, I'll be in trouble, and that's not fair to me").

CONTRIBUTING TO THE COMMON GOOD

ASSET 8: Children as Resources
ASSET 9: Service to Others
ASSET 38: Self-Esteem
ASSET 39: Sense of Purpose

The first step to involving young people in altruistic acts is to believe that they are assets to the home and community. The next step is to observe preteens' individual talents and seek ways to engage them in useful projects that will benefit someone other than themselves. Kids who contribute their time and skills find out they are competent and valued for what they can do.

In a frenzied world, adults often forget that young

people like to be asked for their help and would jump at the chance to contribute to their community. Sometimes, parents do it all themselves because they can do what needs to be done quicker, easier, and more conveniently.

Sometimes, too, kids' appearances (clothing, jewelry, or hairstyles) put adults off. Youth possess an abundance of assets: energy, humor, good will, intelligence, empathy, creativity, loyalty, and sense of fairness. Each preteen possesses his or her own combination of assets and can be a valued resource at home and in the community. All it takes is for parents and other adults to look for and build on the strengths that each child possesses. Kids who can draw can make posters, kids who can write can write letters or provide written information to others, kids who are outgoing can engage others verbally or through drama. The opportunities are endless.

Many schools offer students opportunities to serve the community through service-learning, which connects what students learn in the classroom to real community issues. Kids learning about ecological systems may volunteer as a class to clean up the banks of a local waterway. In order to understand poverty's root causes, classes studying the Great Depression may collect and deliver food and toiletries to a local homeless shelter or food pantry. Many times, kids develop career aspirations after engaging in volunteer work because they find they enjoy the experience and can envision themselves doing it for a living.

❗ Parenting Tips

- *Look at what needs to be done in and around your home on an ongoing basis.* Decide which important jobs you can delegate to your preteens (with your instruction and supervision), based on their interests and talents. Ask them to develop a weekly shopping list by inventorying the cupboards and refrigerator, or ask them to vacuum, do yard work, paint a fence, or do other house chores.

- *Ask your children how they could contribute to your home and to others in the community.* They may have great ideas you haven't thought of, and see community needs from a different perspective. Help them make their ideas a reality.

- *Parents who volunteer in the community teach their kids the value and joy of contribution.* If you volunteer, take your kids along whenever possible. Discuss why you volunteer and what you derive from the experience.

- *Look for ways your whole family can contribute to others:* through holiday gift projects, supporting the local food shelf, donating clothes to charity, bringing food to those who are ill or who have had a death in the family, and helping elderly people in your neighborhood with difficult chores.

COURTESY AND MANNERS

ASSET 26: Caring
ASSET 33: Interpersonal Competence

Can you place the speaker of this statement?

> The children now love luxury. They have bad manners, contempt for authority; they show disrespect for elders and love chatter in place of exercise. Children are now tyrants, not the servants of their households. They no longer rise when elders enter the room. They contradict their parents, chatter before company, gobble up dainties at the table, cross their legs, and tyrannize their teachers.

The speaker is none other than the philosopher Socrates. It seems preteens have been acting up for over two thousand years, and to this day they need parents to teach them good manners. When preteens grow older, having good manners will be an expectation in many areas of their lives. People are simply put off by rude behavior.

Peers often encourage discourteous behavior, thinking it funny or a bit rebellious. Polite preteens may be considered "goody two shoes" or nerdy. Having an "I don't care" attitude may make preteens temporarily popular with peers, but it won't serve them well with teachers, friends' parents, and other adults.

❗ *Parenting Tips*

- *Teach your child to open and hold doors for other people, especially the elderly, disabled, people carrying packages, parents with small children, and others who need assistance.* It is polite and makes sense to wait until the person behind them grasps the door firmly before they let go.

- *Role-play with preteens how to handle introductions with adults.* Encourage them to make steady eye contact, hold out their right hand, and say, "It's nice to meet you"; and answer questions with more than just a yes or no.

- *Explain basic table manners:* Place napkins in the lap. Chew with the mouth closed. Ask for food to be passed instead of reaching. Wait until everyone is served before starting to eat. Thank the person who cooked or paid for dinner.

- *Refrain from criticizing teachers (or other adults) in front of your kids.* Sometimes, preteens think that gives them license to be disrespectful to others.

Teach your children that disagreement with another person doesn't mean they treat that person disrespectfully.

- *Teach preteens to respect others' property:* Ask before borrowing things. Do not walk across neighbors' lawns if asked not to. Pick up litter that has been dropped, instead of ignoring it.

- *Encourage your kids to acknowledge gifts they have received with a thank-you note or phone call.*

- *Teach preteens to bring a simple gift (food, flowers, a game to share) when they're invited to another person's house.*

CRUSHES

ASSET 2: Positive Family Communication
ASSET 11: Family Boundaries
ASSET 31: Healthy Lifestyle

One of the exciting things about growing up is the possibility of having a relationship with someone special. Crushes and dating mark entry into a new set of experiences, pressures, and parental concerns. Every child matures at a different rate. But generally, kids younger than 14 do not have the emotional maturity to handle dating, even though they may have physically matured. Observe your child's behavior and engage in conversations about appropriate behaviors regarding sexuality. Correct inappropriate assumptions and offer accurate information.

You can do a few things now to prepare the way for your children's later successful dating interactions. Let go slowly, and help your preteen get used to spending time in mixed groups of boys and girls with whom he or she is friends. At this age, there is a huge difference between a 12-year-old and a 15-year-old in terms of emotional development, so encourage your child to interact with people in the same age group. When the teen years arrive, your child will be ready.

! *Parenting Tips*

- *When your preteen (around age 11 or 12) begins to express an interest in "going with someone," encourage your preteen to invite groups of friends to your home or to activities that you help to plan, such as skating, movies, dances, and school events.*

- *Do not allow your preteen (boy or girl) to go on dates alone at this age.*

- *If your preteen has a "special interest," allow your child to invite that person to your home and be sure to supervise.* Make sure to introduce yourself to the other preteen's parents and let them know that you will be present when the preteens are in your home.

- *Don't allow your preteen to date an older teen.*

- Preteens may engage in wrestling or other forms of contact because they are curious. *Put a stop to physical activity that you feel is inappropriate.*

- *Talk with your child about the physical, emotional, and cognitive changes that your child is experiencing.* He or she needs the facts and needs to know what you think about sexual activity of all types. Remember that kids often get misinformation from one another and the media.

- *Provide the correct information and structure that reflects your values and will protect them and guide them into adulthood* (parentingteens.about.com).

CURFEWS

ASSET 10: Safety
ASSET 11: Family Boundaries

Preteens generally don't understand why parents won't just let them go where they want and give them their freedom. They almost never think curfews are late enough and almost always believe their friends have it better than they do. But it is important to explain to kids that curfews provide safe boundaries within which they can practice decision-making and social abilities.

To be meaningful, curfews must be relevant to the specific situation. For example, during the school week, a child may need to stay out late for a good reason (a school play or sports game). Occasionally, late nights may happen. Protect school nights to ensure your kids get enough sleep. Allowing kids to stay out late on school nights for recreational purposes communicates a message that school is not important.

Work out a curfew with your preteen that is both reasonable and respectful of the specific activity. This is more effective than setting an inflexible time and expecting your child to deal with it. Negotiating with your kids teaches them cooperation skills and communicates respect for their opinions and needs.

❗ *Parenting Tips*

- *Check with other parents to learn their curfew times for school and weekend nights.* Share your reasoning about your curfews with them. Often, kids convince their parents that all the other parents allow kids out on school nights. Unless you check, you won't be sure. Talking with other parents may help encourage them to make school nights more important, too.

- *Be firm and fair when setting curfews.* If your preteen ignores curfews, enforce consequences firmly to set the tone of importance.

- *Make sure your children understand that adhering to a curfew shows how they are capable of mature behavior, and will help you set later curfews as they grow older.*

- *Don't rely on curfews to be assured of your kids' well-being.* Continue to check to make sure they are where they said they would be.

- *Introduce yourself to parents at homes where your child visits and offer to reciprocate by inviting their child to your home.*

DISCIPLINE

ASSET 2: Positive Family Communication
ASSET 11: Family Boundaries
ASSET 16: High Expectations

As your preteen thinks more abstractly and independently, it's important to calmly discuss the reasons behind family rules. Listen to your child's input, and consider it before responding. As you find just the right balance of letting go and setting boundaries, it can be helpful to reflect on how you were disciplined. Consider parenting practices you didn't find helpful, and retain the techniques that communicated love, provided protection, and established high expectations for behavior.

In his book *WHY Do They Act That Way?*, author David Walsh describes three dominant styles of parenting: permissive, authoritarian, and structured. The permissive style features few rules, few consequences, endless negotiation, erratic leadership, emphasis on individuality, and equal opinions. On the other hand, the authoritarian style has rigid rules, strict enforcement, no negotiation, autocratic leadership, an emphasis on conformity, and consideration only for a parent's opinion. A structured parenting style is marked by firm rules, firm enforcement, limited negotiation, stable leadership, balance, and respect for everyone's opinions.

When dealing with preteens, Walsh says that a structured parenting style is most effective for teaching and protecting them. No matter what kids say and what arguments they present for removing rules, because their brains have not yet fully developed, they still need parents to help them make sound decisions and moderate their behavior.

Don't let yourself be swayed by tears and apologies. It is important for preteens to internalize the consequences of their actions for behavior to change. It is also critical to make your discipline enforceable. In the heat of the moment, you may ground your child for a month and later realize you cannot enforce the punishment for a variety of reasons. Be sure the consequences are appropriate for your child and you don't end up penalizing yourself.

❶ *Parenting Tips*

- *Consistency is critical.* Kids find loopholes in parental behavior. Be consistent with your consequences.

- *Make sure your children know the reasoning behind your rules.*

- *Make sure your kids know which rules are negotiable and which are not.* For instance, wearing bike helmets and seat belts is mandatory, but curfews and chores are negotiable.

- *Listen to the thoughts and reasons behind your child's requests.* If you can negotiate, do so. If not, remain firm and calm, stating your reasons clearly.

- *Focus on the positive during a period of punishment.* When you see your child behaving in ways you believe show maturity or growth, acknowledge it specifically. For instance, "I noticed you left the dinner table and started your homework every night this week without being reminded. That really shows maturity on your part. Good for you." Don't lift the punishment, however; just acknowledge the progress.

- *Renegotiate rules when you notice significant growth in your child's behavior.*

- *If you renegotiate rules, maintain structure and firm enforcement.*

- Relaxing rules may feel risky. *Connect with other parents and discuss their rules and consequences.* You need the support and so do they.

EATING DISORDERS

ASSET 2: Positive Family Communication
ASSET 37: Personal Power

With so much attention focused on body image in TV shows, movies, and magazines, it's little wonder preteens worry about measuring up. Eating disorders are becoming more prevalent and are affecting ever-younger children. According to the National Association of Anorexia Nervosa and Associated Disorders, eating disorders usually start in the teens but may begin as early as age eight. Approximately eight million people in the U.S. have an eating disorder. Ninety percent of those are female, but it is becoming more common to see boys with eating disorders (American Academy of Family Physicians, familydoctor.org).

Anorexia is an obsession with being thin. Those with this eating disorder have a distorted body image, often insisting they are fat even when the scale and mirror say otherwise. Anorexics may severely restrict their calorie intake, exercise excessively, and take diet pills or laxatives. Severe cases require medical intervention, since starving the body affects all internal organs and can result in death if left untreated.

Bulimia, a related eating disorder, involves eating huge amounts of food and then purging food from the body by using laxatives or throwing up. Those with bulimia may also take diet pills to control their weight. People with bulimia are often close to normal weight, but their weight can fluctuate.

With both anorexia and bulimia, serious medical issues are at stake. People who have anorexia are at risk for stomach, heart, and hormonal problems. Often girls experience irregular menstrual periods or no periods at all. Skin becomes dry and scaly, and fine hair grows all over the body, including the face. Those who have bulimia also are at risk for stomach, heart, and kidney problems. In addition, they may have dental problems and dehydration from forced vomiting. Preteens often do not realize the long-term damage done by an eating disorder, since the immediate reward of being thin is so attractive.

❗ *Parenting Tips*

- *Trust your instincts.* If you think your preteen has an eating disorder, follow up on your concerns. Eating disorders are insidious, and if ignored, they can become difficult to treat.

- *Eating disorders are often related to control issues, so avoid an authoritarian attitude with your pre-*

Eating Disorder Warning Signs

- Unnatural concern about body weight
- Obsession with calories, fat, and food
- Use of medicine to prevent weight gain
- Throwing up after meals
- Refusing to eat or lying about how much was eaten
- Fainting
- Over-exercising
- Not having menstrual periods
- Increased anxiety about weight
- Calluses or scars on the knuckle from forced throwing up
- Denying there is a problem (familydoctor.org)

teen. Set firm rules, enforce them firmly, limit negotiation, provide stable family leadership and balance, and respect opinions (Walsh, 2004).

- *Talk to your children about what you are noticing.* Make sure they know that you are concerned for their welfare and that, as a parent, you cannot ignore what you see.

- *Ask for their help in dealing with the problem.*

- *Get counseling from a trusted expert in eating disorders.* Follow through with a behavior plan that your therapist, your child, and you develop together (see "Online Resources" on page 173).

- *If your behavior plan for your preteen is not successful, it is important to seek outpatient or inpatient medical treatment.*

- *Be aware of your own behavior:* Do you obsess about your weight, diet often, or use medication to help control your weight? Do you comment on other people's weight? If necessary, change your behavior for your child's benefit. Encourage healthy relationships with food and teach your child not to skip meals.

- *Correct inaccurate information that your child may have regarding genes, body types and shapes, and average clothing sizes.* Pay attention to anorexia-related deaths of fashion models and other high-profile figures and discuss them openly with your preteen.

GAMBLING

ASSET 11: Family Boundaries
ASSET 31: Healthy Lifestyle

"I bet I can beat you to the door!" "I bet you can't." "I bet a million dollars I can, too!" Sound familiar and pretty innocent? Unfortunately, gambling for money, which is increasingly attracting younger and younger kids, is not. Preteens engage in betting on football or baseball games, card games, or any number of contests. Lottery tickets, perceived by many adults as harmless, are often attractive to kids who can talk others over 18 years old into buying them. Many organizations use gambling activities as fundraisers. Kids may take what adults consider to be innocent fun to the extreme.

Gambling can become an addiction, and, for some young people, can create huge problems, including academic failure, loss of friends, depression, and even suicide. Preteens gamble for a variety of reasons, including peer pressure, and often for the same reasons they may use alcohol, tobacco, or other drugs. Gambling a little, like drinking or smoking a little, may seem harmless, but not all people are capable of remaining moderate.

People who become regular gamblers say they do so for the excitement and enjoyment, not just for money. The adrenaline high connected with winning hooks many people, younger as well as older. Gambling helps them temporarily forget their troubles. Gamblers pursue that feeling even when the financial and emotional costs add up. Be aware of this growing trend in young people and be alert for signs that your son or daughter may have a problem with gambling. If you are concerned that your preteen might have a gambling problem, seek professional help.

The International Centre for Youth Gambling, based at McGill University (www.youthgambling.com), has developed this list of signs of adolescent gamblers:

- *Report beginning gambling at an early age (approximately age 10).*

- *More likely to be boys, although girls are increasingly participating.*

- *Often have parents, relatives, or friends who gamble.*

- *Are overly represented as a group compared to adult gamblers.*

- *Are greater risk takers in general.*

- *Often show signs of lower self-esteem.*

- *Tend to report higher rates of depression.*

- *Often gamble to escape problems.*

- *Are more likely to develop a gambling addiction (or other addictions).*

- *Seem to be more excitable and outgoing.*

- *Are more anxious and less self-disciplined.*

- *Are at greater risk for suicide ideation and suicide attempts.*

- *Often replace their regular friends with gambling acquaintances.*

- *Have poor general coping skills.*

- *Often recall having an early, "big" win.*

- *Report more daily hassles and major traumatic life events.*

- *Are more likely to be delinquent and involved in criminal activities to acquire money.*

- *Develop problems in relationships with family and friends.*

- *Move quickly from occasional gambling with friends and family to addictive or "problem" gambling.*

- *Show decreased academic performance.*

The Illinois Institute for Addiction Recovery (www.addictionrecov.org) offers these additional symptoms of a gambling problem in a young person. You may notice any number of these signs as well in a preteen who gambles:

- *Has an unexplained need for money.*

- *Money or possessions are missing from the home.*

- *Runs up unexplained charges on parents' credit cards.*

- *Withdraws from friends, family, and outside activities and interests.*

- *Misses school or classes and experiences a sudden drop in grades.*

- *Experiences frequent anxiety, depression, or mood swings.*

- *Engages in excessive television watching.*

- *Becomes unreasonably upset at the outcome of a sports match, and shows an interest in sports teams with no previous allegiance.*

- *Makes calls for sports scores and point spreads.*

- *Shows off unexplained wealth.*

! Parenting Tips

- *Keep the lines of communication open.* Listen and pay attention to his concerns. Talk about the risks involved in gambling. Explain that while most people don't develop a gambling addiction, it does happen to some.

- *Point out that gambling is a poor way to make money, and that there is no such thing as instant wealth.*

- *Be aware of your own gambling behaviors.* If visits to casinos or frequent poker games for money are a regular part of your life, realize that your actions are noticed by your preteen.

- *Seek an assessment for your preteen if you are seriously concerned about gambling signs or behaviors.* Help *is* available.

GRIEF

ASSET 1: Family Support
ASSET 2: Positive Family Communication
ASSET 37: Personal Power

Grief occurs as a result of many different losses. Children often experience grief when parents divorce, or when they move away from home and friends to a new city. Preteens grieve deeply when a pet dies. Losing a parent or loved one due to illness, accidental death, or incarceration also can trigger grief, as can losing a dream of becoming a model or making the varsity team.

Grief is a process, not an event. It is real, and it cannot be rushed or pushed away. It is a matter of the heart, not the mind. If kids are not allowed to process their grief, it can have repercussions, including depression and physical or behavior problems.

Unfortunately, there is no shelter from loss. Parents cannot protect children from the pain of loss. But parents *can* support kids through their grief with love, accurate and age-appropriate information, reassurance, and coping strategies. Adults may be better able to process a loss cognitively, but preteens often need help expressing their emotions. Grief shakes their sense of safety and security.

Preteens move through the typical stages of grief— shock, reaction, disruption, and rebuilding—but they may do it differently from adults. Preteens may feel that somehow they caused the loss. Maybe in a moment of anger they wished that the person who died or the parent who yelled at them would just go away, and then that actually happened. Guilt feelings like this are normal. Reassure your kids that everyone has wished things in anger, and that they did not cause the loss by their thoughts.

When a family is shaken by a death, parents sometimes are unable to help a preteen struggling with grief.

How Preteens Express Grief

Psychologist Kimberly Keith offers these signs of preteen grief at childparenting.about.com:

- Physical symptoms (headaches, stomachaches, sleeping and eating disorders, hypochondria), wide mood swings

- Inability to verbally express emotions

- Feelings of helplessness, hopelessness

- Increase in risk-taking, self-destructive behaviors

- Anger, aggression, fighting, oppositional behavior

- Withdrawal from adults

- Depression, sadness

- Lack of concentration and attention

- Identity confusion

- Testing limits.

Ask for help from other caring adults if you aren't able to comfort your child. Grieving behavior in children may be aggravating or inappropriate, especially at a time when everyone else is so upset. While a preteen's response may seem self-centered, it is a normal reaction for a person whose childhood has been disrupted. You can help grieving children in the following ways:

- *Accept that they will experience mood swings and physical symptoms.*

- *Encourage them to recognize their painful feelings and find positive outlets in physical and creative activities.*

- *Listen for the feelings behind their words and actions, and respond with empathy.*

- *Be truthful and factual in explaining the loss.*

- *Help them develop and maintain their sense of identity.*

- *Allow them to make choices that are not harmful.*

- *Encourage safe expressions and experiences of independence* (Kimberly Keith, M.A., L.P.C., childparenting.about.com).

❗ *Parenting Tips*

- *Understand that children between the ages of five and nine years old are starting to think more like adults about death, but still believe it will never happen to anyone they know or love.* They may be in shock.

- *It is normal for preteens to feel immediate grief after a loss.*

- *Preteens may feel sad off and on over a long period of time.* Eventually, normal sadness will pass.

- *Make sure kids know it is okay to feel happy again and they need not feel guilty.*

- *If your preteen is not comfortable attending a funeral, don't force the issue.* Consider doing something else with her to honor the person's memory.

- *A good way for children to process grief is to create a memory box in which special things associated with the person are placed.* Discuss what she chooses to put in the box and why.

- *Lighting candles, making a scrapbook, reviewing photos, and saying a prayer are all ways to help preteens express feelings of grief.*

- *Anticipate special dates (like the anniversary of a loss, a birthday, or other special occasion) and be with your child on those days to mark the occasion in a hopeful way.*

- *Answer questions honestly.* Try to address fears about illness or hospitals if they arise. Children might fear that everyone who goes to the hospital will die of illness. Assure them that many people get well and leave the hospital feeling better.

- *If your child needs help coping with grief, seek counseling.* According to the Web site of the American Academy of Child and Adolescent Psychiatry (www.aacap.org), a child's long-term denial or avoidance of grief can be a sign of a serious problem. When children experience difficulty with grief, they may become depressed, lose interest in daily activities, be unable to sleep, lose their appetite, not want to be alone, act younger than their age, excessively imitate or want to join the dead person, withdraw from friends, or experience a drop in academic performance. Pediatricians, school counselors, and hospice organizations can all provide referrals to grief counselors.

LEARNING STYLES AND MULTIPLE INTELLIGENCES

ASSET 5: Caring School Climate
ASSET 21: Achievement Motivation

Harvard University professor Howard Gardner, author of *Frames of Mind: The Theory of Multiple Intelligences*

(1983), asserts that there are at least eight "intelligences" or ways in which people are smart. Schools (and standardized tests) generally focus on only two of those areas: the verbal-linguistic and logical-mathematical intelligences. Unfortunately, for students who excel in other areas of intelligence—spatial, bodily-kinesthetic, musical, interpersonal, intrapersonal, and naturalist—the ways they learn best are not generally nurtured by schools. Some students may gradually become convinced they are not intelligent, when what they really need is to be taught in other ways.

A musically intelligent child might learn new information in social studies or math much more readily if the facts are delivered through musical patterns. This could entail setting historical facts to familiar music or writing a song based on math concepts. An interpersonally-intelligent child remembers facts better when they are related to human elements. She might engage more effectively with the topic of the Civil War by being asked to consider the impact of slavery on the parents whose children were taken away.

Several tools are available for teachers and parents to determine how preteens learn best and more readily engage them in active learning. Gardner suggests that delivering new information to students through the avenue of their strongest intelligence helps ensure their academic engagement.

Most people have a preferred style of learning. Many preteens do best when they can see what the teacher is talking about. Graphs, picture, diagrams, and maps help visual learners best. Some children learn well by simply listening. They may hear something spoken and, if it's meaningful, will remember it. These are the auditory learners. Still others learn by doing. They are hands-on, or kinesthetic, learners.

Learning is enhanced for everyone when new

material is offered in a variety of ways: visually, aurally (through hearing), and kinesthetically (through movement). Understanding how your child learns best and how your child is intelligent can help you communicate effectively with teachers to make sure your preteen stays engaged and motivated. When you respect, nurture, and utilize children's unique intelligences and learning styles, you increase their motivation to learn and their hope in a positive future.

! *Parenting Tips*

- *Learn about the multiple intelligences and help your preteens understand how they are smart.* Encourage them to learn more on their own (see "Online Resources" on page 173).

- *Observe your kids doing things they really enjoy.* Note the activities they naturally seem to choose, and plan outings and gifts around those choices.

- *Ask your preteen to think about the ways in which his favorite public personalities are intelligent* (for example, elite athletes are bodily-kinesthetically intelligent, while many popular singers and musicians are musically intelligent). Encourage your child to identify and develop his strongest intelligences and find ways to support them.

- *Don't expect teachers to always teach to your child's strongest intelligence.* If school problems do arise, communicate calmly with teachers and explain how your child learns best. Look for clues in his misbehavior. Excessive talking in class may indicate strong verbal or interpersonal skills in your preteen, which could be channeled in more productive ways, such as speaking in front of class or greeting new students. Artistic doodling may indicate strong spatial intelligence and indicate what a child knows about a topic. Excessive fidgeting may indicate boredom or the need to get up and move. Being allowed to stand or walk (without disrupting others) may actually help increase a kinesthetic learner's attention span.

MATERIAL POSSESSIONS

ASSET 11: Family Boundaries
ASSET 30: Responsibility

You may hear people observe that kids today have more material possessions than *they* ever had and feel justly entitled to them. In our consumer-driven society, kids and parents are sometimes too easily swayed by advertising and a need to keep pace with other families' spending habits, as well as a desire to provide well for the family.

It is tempting to give in to children's pleas for things that undermine parental values in order to appease them and earn their devotion. Blaming children for their lack of understanding regarding money and what it costs to earn that money is not warranted. When they haven't yet had a chance to earn their own money, preteens' frame of reference is necessarily different from ours. They need you to give them opportunities to experience a different way of looking at the subject.

❗ *Parenting Tips*

- *Let your child handle and care for his own money.* Instead of handing out money every time it's asked for, try regularly giving a set amount. Ask him to keep track of how he spends it, and discuss the choices he makes. Don't give out more if your child spends it all before the next scheduled payout. That will negate the lesson you are trying to teach and reinforce any sense of entitlement your child may feel.

- *Do some simple arithmetic with your child.* How many hours would a person have to work to earn $20 at the minimum wage? Remind your preteen that an employer also withholds part of every paycheck for taxes.

- *Ask your child to do age-appropriate chores, not as a way to earn money but because she is a valued member of the family.* Contributing time and effort to the smooth running of the household is what family members do to ensure the family's success.

- *Discuss the importance of caring for possessions.* Picking up clothes and placing CDs in their cases are just two examples; don't replace items that aren't properly cared for.

- *Remember that it's normal for kids to ask for things.* Instead of becoming exasperated and making him feel guilty for asking, calmly discuss the costs and help him develop a savings plan that allows him to work toward a goal. Guiding preteens now toward becoming financially savvy contributes to their later successes in handling money as adults.

MOODINESS AND DEPRESSION

ASSET 37: Personal Power
ASSET 38: Self-Esteem
ASSET 40: Positive View of Personal Future

When a preteen becomes depressed, parents may not immediately recognize the signs. Depression in children and teens can result from altered brain chemistry or be related to environmental and emotional issues, or both.

The behaviors that parents initially observe may seem like moodiness or acting out rather than depression. When parents do recognize what their child is experiencing, they may feel guilty or responsible in some way for their child's unhappiness. To help a depressed child, it is important for parents to become educated and seek help immediately. Untreated preteen depression may lead to serious problems, including substance abuse, eating disorders, and suicide. But with treatment, depression can be managed well.

Personal power and self-esteem assets are critical in managing or resolving depression. Depressed individuals do not feel in control of their lives, feel bad about themselves, and often withdraw socially. It is difficult to hold a positive view of one's future when depressed.

Most people have experienced feelings of sadness at one time or another and may even have used the word *depressed* to describe their feelings. However, a true clinical diagnosis of depression depends on a cluster of specific symptoms lasting at least two weeks (Swartz, 2001). Uma Rao, M.D., and Kathy Swartz, M.D., writing in *The Prevention Researcher,* offer these key signs of depression in preteen children:

- *Depressed or irritable mood, social withdrawal, behavior problems*

- *Decreased interest or pleasure in activities*

- *Change in appetite, weight, or vitality*

- *Sleeping more or less than usual*

- *Fatigue or loss of energy*

- *Feelings of guilt or worthlessness*

- *Decreased concentration, poor school attendance or performance, indecision*

- *Sense of hopelessness*

- *Substance abuse*

- *Recurrent thoughts of death or suicide*

- *Substance abuse, reported by 30–50 percent of depressed youth* (Swartz, 2001 and Rao, 2001).

Sadness is *not* depression. Feelings of sadness are appropriate for certain circumstances. The death of a pet or loved one, the loss of a friend who moves away, or disruptions in family relationships can cause feelings of sadness that may last a few days or more. When sadness lasts for a few weeks and is accompanied by any number of symptoms mentioned above, it is important for parents to intervene.

In addition, it is helpful for parents to realize that depression looks different in preteens than in adults. And often, depressed youth show signs of agitation, rather than lethargy. Behavioral problems may mask depression. But depression is a treatable illness. Cognitive and behavioral therapy (and sometimes medication) can successfully restore a preteen's quality of life.

ⓘ Parenting Tips

- *Note the behaviors that concern you and determine how long the behaviors have been going on, how often they occur, and how severe they seem.*

- *Talk to trusted friends or family members to verify your perceptions.*

- *Listen to your preteen.* If she makes statements like "No one likes me" or "I am just no good," determine if she is just having a bad day or if she truly feels this way about herself. Note how often she says things like this. If you hear this often, seek counseling for her.

- *Don't blame yourself.* Focus instead on providing support to your child and yourself as well.

- *Get accurate information from the library, help lines, the Internet, and other sources.* Ask questions about treatments and services.

- *See a mental health professional or your child's doctor for evaluation and diagnosis.* Look for a mental health professional who specializes in treating children and teenagers.

- *The diagnostic evaluation may include psychological testing, laboratory tests, and consultation with other medical specialists such as a child and adolescent psychiatrist.* A comprehensive treatment plan may include psychotherapy, ongoing evaluations and monitoring, or psychiatric medication. Optimally, decisions about treatment involve the preteen and his or her parents

- *Advocate for your child.* Sometimes it takes a few tries to find the right therapist and the right medication and dosage (if appropriate). If you aren't satisfied with your preteen's response to treatment, get another opinion. Sometimes children need to try several medications before finding one that works. Parents and physician need to stay in close communication. Every person's brain chemistry is unique. Partner with your prescribing doctor by telling him or her what you observe when your preteen takes a new medication.

- *Puberty affects medication.* If your preteen is taking medication before puberty, the dosage or medication may need adjustment when puberty arrives.

- *Join a family support group organized by such organizations as the National Alliance on Mental Illness* (www.nami.org).

OUTBURSTS AND ANGER

ASSET 2: Positive Family Communication
ASSET 11: Family Boundaries
ASSET 14: Adult Role Models
ASSET 36: Peaceful Conflict Resolution

In a given day, a preteen's mood can swing from happy to sad to angry—multiple times. For a parent, it may be very difficult to deal with an angry preteen. You may not understand what provoked the anger or the intensity of the reaction to something you perceive as less than catastrophic. Preteens are expert at simultaneously pushing you away and pulling you to them. It is important to keep your cool and react in ways that de-escalate, rather than exacerbate, the situation.

Preteens believe the world revolves around them and may think no one can possibly understand how they feel. They believe everyone is looking at them and judging their every move. They need to feel that they are in control, performing well. When circumstances turn out other than they hoped, they react with anger that belies their immaturity and lack of resources to deal effectively with whatever happened.

Underlying anger is often disappointment, hurt, embarrassment, loss of control, or failure of some kind. Depression is not uncommon in preteens, who often exhibit different behavioral symptoms of depression from adults. Inability to sleep may manifest itself as staying up too late watching TV. Inability to concentrate may show up in a drop in grades. "Adolescent depression may also present primarily as a behavior or conduct disorder, substance or alcohol abuse, or as family turmoil and rebellion with no obvious symptoms reminiscent of depression," says Canadian psychiatrist Maurice Blackman (www.mentalhealth.com).

Preteens do not possess the life experiences or brain maturity to enable them to fully identify or understand their feelings. They demonstrate anger when other feelings may be present that they need to address. Realize that, as the adult, your responsibility is to rise above the situation in order to defuse it. Avoid reacting to anger with more anger or minimizing the situation by saying, "What could you possibly have to be so upset about?" An angry preteen's brain is on high alert. Adrenaline is pumping, and there is little or no access to the reasoning part of the brain.

Offer nonjudgmental support and communicate your love and understanding. Kids are more likely to open up to parents if they know you'll listen quietly in a nonjudgmental way, and refrain from adding your opinions and suggestions immediately. The ability to manage anger is a critical life skill. Those who hold anger in are more prone to depression; self-injury; risk-taking behaviors; alcohol, tobacco, and other drug use; and eating disorders.

Learning to manage anger starts with allowing kids to be angry. If you are uncomfortable with anger or angry people, you may try to put a stop to anger before it is adequately resolved. Kids need to feel their emotions, identify the circumstances that trigger them, and then learn what to do with them.

Adults sometimes mistakenly take for granted that kids can correctly identify their emotions. It is important for kids to learn to name their feelings and where they feel those emotions physically. Many kids have stomachaches or headaches when they are emotionally upset. Recognizing physical feelings is the first step in dealing effectively with them.

In many cases, preteens can work through their emotions on their own. However, intervene immediately if your child is being physically destructive (hitting or breaking things) or verbally abusive to others. Everyone's physical and emotional safety comes first. Physical or verbal abuse by a preteen is extreme behavior that indicates a serious problem and one that needs intervention by trained professionals.

Because preteens have limited life experience, they may react to disappointment or frustration with anger more often than not. Not being chosen for the team? Anger. Not getting invited to the party? Anger. A bad grade? Anger. How can you help them understand what they're feeling? By listening to what they say, rather than focusing on the anger, and by reflecting back what they say and helping them understand their feelings. Be sure to name the emotion: "I know you're feeling very upset about your grade. You worked so hard. Do you think you may be feeling as disappointed as you are angry? Maybe we can figure out how you could do better next time."

"In a recent study mapping differences between the brains of adults and teens, Deborah Yurgelun-Todd put teenage and adult volunteers through an MRI and monitored how their brains responded to a series of pictures. The volunteers were asked to discern the emotion on a series of faces. The results were surprising. All the adults identified the emotion as fear, but many of the teenagers saw something different, such as shock or anger. When she examined their brain scans, Yurgelun-Todd found that the teenagers were using a different part of their brain when reading the images" (www.pbs.org).

Many effective approaches are available for managing preteen anger. Teach your child to try a number of the following strategies:

- **Think It Out**—Take time to sit outside or lie on a bed and think about what happened. Put it into perspective. What are you feeling along with the anger? How important is it really? What could you do now? How can you avoid it happening again?

- **Talk It Out**—Talk with a friend, parent, or even a dog or cat about what upset you.

- **Write It Out**—Journal, scribble, or draw your feelings.

- **Work It Out**—Do something physical—walk, run, hit a ball, take a bath or shower, or punch a pillow (pbskids.org/itsmylife/).

- **Plan It Out**—Devising a plan for action gives a preteen a feeling of control. Planning what to do next time, no matter what the issue, teaches preteens that all is not lost, that they have control over their actions, and they can affect what happens in the future.

❗ *Parenting Tips*

- *Calmly acknowledge that your child is very angry:* "Wow! I can see you're pretty upset. Is there anything I can do?"
- *Offer to do something physical:* "Do you want to take a walk (shoot baskets, punch a pillow)?"

- *Give your preteen some space:* "Listen, I can see you need some time alone. Why don't you go upstairs for a bit? Do you want something to eat or drink?"

Spotlight on Social-Competencies Assets

Preteens need good role models, good listeners, and good parent-teachers who will help them develop social competence. People who can identify and manage their feelings are emotionally intelligent. According to Daniel Goleman, author of *Emotional Intelligence: Why It Can Matter More Than IQ,* emotional IQ is more important in life than intellectual IQ. Being able to manage one's own feelings and also interact competently with other people are skills that spell life-long success.

- *When your preteen has calmed down, gently ask what happened.* Listen without judgment. Paraphrase to check for understanding. It might sound like this: "So, you found out at lunch that the boy you like has been calling your friend and she didn't tell you." or "You failed the math test and you're really upset."

- *Respond with compassion:* "I can see how that would really hurt." Don't minimize or accuse. Avoid saying, "You'll get over it" or "If you'd studied harder, this wouldn't have happened."

- *Help your child identify the underlying feeling:* "So you got mad because your feelings were hurt. I can really understand that." (Refrain from telling your own stories at this point unless your preteens ask. This is their crisis.) Listen, and let there be silence if that is what happens.

- *Avoid discouraging crying for girls and boys.* Allow preteens to express their hurt feelings verbally and, if tears come, acknowledge that tears are a good release for emotional pain.

- *When your child is calm (this may be hours later or even the next day), move into the problem-solving phase:* "So, what will you say to your friend when you see her tomorrow? How will you act?" or "So, what can you do to make this situation better? Do you understand what went wrong? Can you ask for a make-up test? Can you create a better plan for studying for the next test?"

PIERCING AND TATTOOS

ASSET 11: Family Boundaries
ASSET 31: Healthy Lifestyle

Tattoos and body piercings are everywhere: on athletes, music stars, actors, and older teens. It is understandable that preteens may also want one just like the favorite role models they admire. It is critical to consider various issues involved with tattooing and piercing for your preteen's own safety, including physical health risks and public perceptions. Discuss these concerns honestly with your preteens and help them understand that some fashion trends carry long-term risks.

 Parenting Tips

- *Determine your own values regarding tattoos and piercings.* What messages do they communicate? How do you feel about people who have them? When, if ever, do you think a child is old enough for a piercing or a tattoo?

- *Are you clear with your opinion so that if your preteen asks for permission to get a tattoo or piercing, you know what your response will be?* Base your answer to your child on facts, rather than on an impulsive reaction.

- *Your preteen should know that procedures that involve puncturing the skin (tattoos and piercings) carry health risks, including infection (and disease transmission, if performed improperly).*

- *Make sure your child knows that piercings take a long time (sometimes months) to heal and that proper wound care is important.* Piercings close eventually, but not without scarring. And both piercings and tattoos are meant to be permanent. It is possible to remove a tattoo, but it's slow, painful, and costly.

- *Remember that kids can't necessarily think through or anticipate the consequences of their actions.* Respect their request, engage them in an informed discussion, and offer the facts as you explain, no matter which answer you give. Help your child see that these are big decisions.

- *Act on your beliefs.* If you believe your preteen is too young for piercings or tattoos, maintain your boundaries.

PUBERTY

ASSET 2: Positive Family Communication
ASSET 37: Personal Power
ASSET 38: Self-Esteem

Puberty is a time of excitement and change for some kids, and upheaval and uncertainty for others. While some move through puberty relatively unscathed, others turn their worlds, and yours, upside down. Preteens (and their parents) often wonder how tall they'll be, where their voices will finally settle, and what their hair will eventually look like. It is a time of mysterious and maturing thoughts and unpredictable emotions.

Some preteens will ask questions related to puberty before you bring up the topic. But you don't have to wait to be asked. Start talking with your kids about puberty beginning around the time they turn eight years old. Normal puberty begins between the ages of 8 and 13 years old for girls and 9 and 14 years old for boys. Puberty is considered late or delayed if it has not begun before age 13 for girls and age 14 for boys.

Kids want to be able to ask parents questions about their changing bodies without feeling embarrassed or afraid, and to have your understanding as they adjust to dramatic physical changes like gangly legs, hair growth, larger feet, new breasts, and defined waistlines. Boys and girls also need to know where parents stand on issues related to sexuality and sexual behavior. Talking to your children about sex is important. They need information from a trusted source—you—not just their peers. Preteens also want to know what behaviors you consider appropriate for them. Give them information now to help them make responsible choices later when the time arises. Talk about how pregnancy happens, what sexually transmitted diseases (STDs) are, and how irresponsible sexual behavior can affect a person's health and reputation.

Precocious Puberty

Early puberty is on the rise in the United States and other countries, although no one knows why with certainty. Some experts suspect the reason lies in hormone additives in food, or in insecticides or other environmental causes, as well as an increase in overall body fat and obesity.

Heavier girls seem to menstruate earlier than thin ones. Writer Jennifer Haupt notes, "More young girls are showing signs of puberty as early as 7 or 8 and beginning to menstruate two to three years later. As a result, parents are increasingly faced with the difficult task of talking to young children about topics that

Stages of Puberty in Girls

- Breast development (average age is 10½ years), usually accompanied by a growth spurt.

- Pubic hair development (usually six months after breasts start to develop, but may start before breasts do), followed by axillary hair growth.

- Development of perspiration and body odors, and possibly acne.

- Continued breast, pubic hair, and external genitalia growth over next two years.

- First period (menarche) at the average age of 12½ to 13 years. This usually coincides with a peak in height growth.

- Full development takes approximately three to four years. Two years after menarche, most girls will have reached full height and breast size. (Vincent Iannelli, M.D., pediatrics.about.com)

had traditionally been reserved for preteens and teens" (archives.cnn.com).

When girls start to develop breasts or pubic hair before the age of eight, or when boys start to develop larger testicles or grow pubic hair before the age of nine, they are considered to be in a phase of precocious puberty. For some children, this can be both emotionally and physically difficult and can be a sign of an underlying health problem requiring investigation and medical treatment. Another concern is that, when puberty ends, height growth also ends. Children who enter puberty early and end it too soon may not reach their full height potential. It's important to pinpoint causes of early puberty and treat it appropriately.

Stages of Puberty in Boys

- Increased testicle size (average age is 11½ to 12 years old).

- Growth of pubic hair a few months later.

- Continued growth of testicles, penis, pubic, and axillary hair.

- A peak in growth two to three years later than girls.

- Hands, feet, arms, legs, trunk, and chest continue to grow.

- Voice deepens and muscle mass increases.

- Ability to get erections and ejaculate (nighttime "wet dreams").

- Full development takes about three to four years to reach adult testicle and penis size and pubic hair pattern, followed by the growth of chest and facial hair.

- Puberty also can signal the start of perspiration and body odor and acne (Vincent Iannelli, M.D., pediatrics.about.com).

In addition to coping with the physical effects of precocious puberty, children who go through puberty early may experience teasing from other children. Their changing bodies can embarrass them, and their self-esteem may suffer, leading to a loss of interest in daily activities and to academic or social problems. The good news is that precocious puberty can be treated with medications that stop early production of sex hormones. With parental support and encouragement, kids who experience this condition can do well. If your child has entered early puberty, you can help by explaining what's happening, and provide support and reassurance that things will eventually be fine.

❗ *Parenting Tips*

- *Puberty is normal.* Talking about menarche or nocturnal wet dreams may be a bit uncomfortable for you at first, but your children are likely to appreciate any information you can give them about their changing bodies and practical ways to deal with the changes. Kids may need time to process what you say and will ask more questions later. Don't assume one explanation will be enough.

- *Use teachable moments to relate accurate information, opinions, values, and expectations to your preteens.*

- *Offer accurate information when your preteens ask you questions about sexual matters, and use adult language when you answer them.*

- *Physical sexual development is separate from emotional or cognitive sexual development.* Helping girls and boys understand and handle the sexual urges that accompany their physical development is important. Their bodies will complete the process of puberty long before their ability to handle sexual relationships is fully mature.

- *Let your preteen know there are many ways to express intimacy and attraction.* Spending time getting to know another person and holding hands are both appropriate ways to show someone you are attracted to them.

- *Celebrate the milestones that your child is experiencing.* Acknowledge the changes that you see and provide your child with encouragement when he or she is unhappy with a new, unfamiliar body. Help your child embrace and welcome body changes and new abilities. Focus on the positive aspects of your child's physical appearance and other positive accomplishments.

- *Be observant of outward signs of puberty.* If it's too early, according to the average guidelines, seek advice from your pediatrician. For children experiencing precocious puberty, offer information gently. Children under eight years old do not need dating advice, but they do need to know what is happening to their bodies and why. Reassure them that they are okay and that everyone eventually will go through the changes they are going through now.

SCHOOL STRUGGLES

ASSET 6: Parent Involvement in Schooling
ASSET 22: Learning Engagement
ASSET 40: Positive View of Personal Future

Children who struggle in school may have special needs that are not being met. When a child consistently struggles with school tasks, there may be a developmental reason for it. Many kids seem to be quite intelligent but yet do not perform well in one or more areas. This is the time to investigate and provide support to help your child achieve success and remain committed to learning. Children who experience success in school are more likely to have a positive view of their future—they know that they can accomplish what they set their minds to do.

Your child's teacher, the school psychologist, and guidance counselor are all good sources to consult if your preteen is not performing well. Don't assume your child's failure to perform successfully in school is related to a lack of motivation until you've thoroughly investigated the situation. Remember that learning is as natural as growing, and when learning stops progressing, something is wrong. Kids who are frustrated or fearful about not succeeding academically often misbehave to divert attention from their lack of success. According to Alan Mendler, Ph.D., author of *Discipline with Dignity,* kids often believe it's better to be bad than stupid. Misbehavior can become a way of saving face to divert attention from poor grades.

Learning disabilities (or differences) may be one reason for lack of school success. They are permanent disorders affecting the way individuals with normal or above-normal intelligence receive, store, organize, retrieve, and use information. People with learning disabilities are sometimes regarded as lazy, unmotivated, careless, or unintelligent. It is enormously frustrating for a child to try to do well, but be academically unsuccessful because of an invisible and misunderstood disability.

Children with learning disabilities may exhibit a wide range of traits, including problems with reading comprehension, spoken language, writing, or reasoning ability. Other traits that may be present include uneven and unpredictable test scores, perceptual impairments, motor disorders, and behaviors such as impulsiveness, easily becoming frustrated, and problems with social interactions (National Dissemination Center for Children with Disabilities, nichcy.org).

School psychologists are trained to administer tests that help identify problem areas. But it's parents who make a formal request to the school district for diagnostic testing. If you're reluctant to request testing for fear your child will be labeled, it's important to know that a diagnosis is necessary to ensure your child receives proper support and the academic interventions necessary to be successful in school. When a learning disorder diagnosis is given, a team of school professionals will work together with you to develop an individualized education plan (IEP) for your child.

You might need to ask for additional modifications for your preteen if those offered don't seem to be in your child's best interests. It's essential that you be able to cooperate and communicate effectively with school professionals. Document your communications, and strive to keep a cool head. If your school district is not responsive to your child's needs, have your preteen tested privately, and then work with a special tutor to develop necessary learning strategies for her or him. Every child can learn successfully with the proper support. Advocating for your preteen's best interests can be exhausting and frustrating, but your persistence will pay off and make an enormous difference in your child's life.

❗ *Parenting Tips*

- *Focus on what your child can do.* Point out his or her strengths. For instance, "You really can draw well. I've noticed some terrific pictures in your room."

- *Provide structure and high expectations* (specific times for homework, use of checklists, and homework organizers). Stick to a schedule because predictability is important to a child with a learning disability.

- *Advocate for your child with teachers.* If your preteen is spending too much time on homework, request an adjustment in assignments. Make sure that the IEP is reasonable. Then ensure that your son or daughter does the assignment.

- *Explain your child's learning style and traits to teachers.* If your child needs to get up and move around periodically, encourage the teacher to allow this. Teachers and students can develop a signal that doesn't call attention to the student. For example, when your student makes eye contact with the teacher and scratches his head, the teacher knows he needs to get up and move. Help your child understand that, in order to work, this arrangement cannot be abused.

- *Depending on whether your preteen has difficulty with reading, writing, or math, ask for an alternate assessment method for your child to demonstrate what he knows* (draw, record, or graph it).

- *If your child receives an IEP, make sure teachers are familiar with necessary accommodations that need to be made (give extended work or test time, read the questions aloud, offer an alternate test location).* Parents are the best advocates for their children until children are old enough and confident enough to advocate for themselves.

SEPARATION AND DIVORCE

ASSET 1: Family Support
ASSET 2: Positive Family Communication
ASSET 14: Adult Role Models
ASSET 40: Positive View of Personal Future

When parents separate or divorce, preteens face significant challenges and stresses: seeing one parent less than the other, missing grandparents, shuttling back and forth between two homes, leaving friends, changing schools and needing to make new friends, and adjusting to a parent's new partner, spouse, and relatives, to name just a few.

Today, about half of all marriages end in divorce, and the impact on children can be serious. During a divorce, parents struggle with their own hurt, disappointment, anger, fear, and uncertainty about the future. As a result, it may be difficult to manage even the regular ups and downs of preteens' behaviors. Kids often believe that a divorce or separation was their fault and that they have a responsibility to try to bring the parents back together again.

Parents need to be alert to signs of distress in their children. Younger preteens may react to the divorce by becoming aggressive, uncooperative, or withdrawn. Older preteens may feel deep sadness and loss, and their schoolwork and behavior may suffer.

❗ *Parenting Tips*

- *Never use the children as bargaining tools or to inflict pain on your ex-spouse or partner.*

- *Counseling may be beneficial in order to gather support for yourself and your kids.*

- *Avoid long custody battles or pressuring a child to choose one parent over the other.*

- *Do not vent your anger or feelings on your child. You are the adult.* To feel secure, your child needs you to show that you can manage and everyone will be okay.

- *Allow your preteen his feelings.* He may be angry and need a safe place to express that anger. Stay calm and try to explain your actions in a way they can understand. Sometimes kids get angry at the person they are closest to and feel safest with.

- *Avoid blaming your ex-partner or ex-spouse.*

Talking to Children about Separation and Divorce

The following tips from the American Academy of Child and Adolescent Psychiatry can help both kids and parents with the challenge and stress of talking about separation and divorce:

- Don't keep the separation or divorce a secret.

- Together, tell your kids the news.

- Keep things simple and straightforward.

- Tell children the situation is not their fault.

- Acknowledge that the changes are sad and upsetting for everyone.

- Reassure preteens that you both still love them and will always be their parents.

- Don't discuss each other's faults or problems with the kids (www.aacap.org).

- *If your child must live alternately in two different homes, prepare her for what a new home will be like.* Help her stay organized by providing staples (underwear, toiletries, school supplies, comforting items, and toys) in each home.

- *Make sure that rules in each home are as similar as possible for important issues such as schoolwork, chores, curfew, supervision, and friends.*

- *Work cooperatively with your ex-partner or ex-spouse for the good of your kids.*

SEXUALITY

ASSET 2: Positive Family Communication
ASSET 14: Adult Role Models
ASSET 31: Healthy Lifestyle
ASSET 32: Planning and Decision Making
ASSET 35: Resistance Skills
ASSET 38: Self-Esteem

Sexuality is complex, encompassing much more than the physical act of having sex. It involves how people perceive and express themselves, interact with members of either sex, and form and sustain intimate relationships. Children form positive attitudes toward sexuality when they observe respectful human interaction, clear communication, and care for others modeled by adults around them.

It may seem that preteens are too young to think about these issues, but sexuality has actually been a part of their lives since birth. By two years, most children identify themselves according to their sex. They have started to notice differences in physiology. Most parents have begun socializing children according to accepted norms for their gender.

Children learn about sexuality from what they see and hear parents and other adults do and say. In today's exploitative culture, which uses sex to sell products from beer, cell phones, and cars to popular music, clothes, and vacation destinations, parents must examine the messages preteens absorb from this exposure. How will preteens sort out what is okay and what is not? Do they have sound values to fall back on and a filter through which they can interpret these messages?

Print and electronic media regularly portray casual sex as the norm, often leaving out the negative results of such behavior, including unplanned pregnancy, STDs, and HIV infection. Children need to see models of people who calmly work out relationship issues with a genuine concern for one another's well-being. Unfortunately, media messages frequently emphasize having sex as the "cool" thing to do, and sexual relationships are dealt with superficially. It is important for parents to counterbalance irresponsible sexual messages that preteens receive from movies, TV, their peers, and popular music with well-informed and thoughtful messages of their own.

❗ Parenting Tips

- *Join your children when they are watching TV or movies or listening to music.* Take note when sexually explicit messages are expressed. Ask questions in a calm tone that will help your child question what he or she is seeing and hearing. For example, "Do you think it's realistic to act like that?" "Do you see kids doing that?" "Would you let someone treat you that way?" "Do you wonder why only the fun parts of this behavior are shown, while you never see anyone getting hurt?" Listen to your preteen's responses, and share your own opinions.

- *Talk about the fact that sexuality is not just about having sex—it's about caring relationships, respectful sharing, and good communication.*

- *Make sure your children know what behavior you expect from them.* For example, "I hope you will make good choices. I'd be very disappointed otherwise, because you know what I expect from you."

- *Children need to appreciate their bodies and know that the way they are made is just right for them.* Avoid comparing them to others who are thinner, prettier, more athletic, or more muscular. Point out their unique assets and help them make the most of them.

- *Help your preteen make clothing choices that are not seductive or in a style that's too mature for her age.*

- *Learn what kids in your community are doing sexually.* School counselors are great sources of information. Ask what they know about sexual activity in their school.

- *Be conscious of your own attitudes and behavior in front of your children regarding sexuality.* Do you perpetuate stereotypes? Do you flirt to get what you want? Do you make sexually suggestive comments? Do you make derogatory statements about one sex or the other?

- *It is important for preteens to know that forced sex is a serious crime.* Teach them that it is wrong for anyone (peers, older teens, or adults) to force them into sexual activity of any kind. If it happens, they should report it to you immediately, and you both can alert the authorities. Let them know that no means no, and they always have the right to feel safe.

- *Examine the relationships you model in the way you treat your partner, spouse, and other adults.* Are you respectful, considerate, and understanding?

Sexual Orientation

Sexual orientation, which refers to a person's primary sexual attraction, begins to emerge by adolescence. Some gay and lesbian people report knowing that they felt same-sex attraction by age 10 or 11. It is estimated that between three and 10 percent of the population is homosexual, and another 10 percent is attracted to both sexes, or is bisexual.

If your child announces an attraction to someone of the same sex, you may be comfortable with the announcement, or you may feel conflicted. Parents sometimes blame themselves or wonder what they might have done differently in raising their child. Seek counseling if you find it difficult to deal with your feelings or with your need to reconcile beliefs with your love for your child. Organizations such as Parents, Families, and Friends of Lesbians and Gays (PFLAG) can provide support and information (see "Online Resources" on page 173.) Regardless of the attraction your child feels, use this time as an opportunity to bond more closely with your preteen and develop a relationship based on love, honesty, and trust—all kids deserve no less.

❗ *Parenting Tips*

- *Listen without judgment, hug your child, and ask what your child needs from you besides love and acceptance* (for example, help dealing with teasing at school, counseling, or a support group).

Family therapist Michael Gurian writes in *The Wonder of Boys,* "Scientific evidence pioneered by brain researchers at the University of Pennsylvania and the UCLA School of Medicine and in England, at the London Institute of Psychiatry, makes it clear being gay is not just 'a life-style choice.' It is genetically and chromosomally influenced, with certain families having far more homosexuals in their generational lineage than others; and it is wired into the brain. This wiring has been measured by researchers on autopsied brains. The genetic tendency toward homosexuality and the smaller nucleus in the brain of a gay person are biological facts" (Gurian, 1996).

- *Remember that your child needs you now more than ever and needs to know that he or she is loved and supported.* Without love and support, gay and lesbian kids may suffer from poor self-image and depression, and are at higher risk for substance abuse and sometimes suicide.

- *Encourage your child to be selective when talking about matters related to sexuality and sexual identity.* Sometimes peers are too immature to confide in and can be cruel when someone is perceived as different.

- *Refrain from telling your child that he or she is just going through a stage.*

SLEEP NEEDS

ASSET 1: Family Support
ASSET 11: Family Boundaries
ASSET 31: Healthy Lifestyle

The sleep needs of preteens baffle many parents. Why is it so difficult for them to sleep as well as they did when they were younger? According to researchers, everyone has an internal clock (the circadian rhythm) that changes at various stages of life. Sleep researchers who tested a group of 10- to 12-year-olds discovered that

> after centuries of assuming the longer we are awake, the sleepier we will become and the more we will tend to fall asleep, we were confronted by the surprising result that after 12 hours of being awake, the subjects were less sleepy than they had been earlier in the same day, and at 10 o'clock, after more that 14 hours of wakefulness had elapsed . . . they were even less sleepy (www.pbs.org).

Sleep researchers found that just before puberty, the preteen biological clock opposed the sleep-wakefulness cycle and helped preteens stay alert at night when they should have been falling asleep. Interestingly, when preteens become teens, they need more sleep—nine and one quarter hours per night.

If kids didn't have to go to school or work, it would be easy to adjust to their changing sleep patterns. However, schools often start very early, and that means many preteens are not getting the sleep they need. They

Why Do Kids Need Their Sleep?

"Because most growth hormones throughout the body are especially active during sleep, it is thought that the majority of neurotrophic work is also done during sleep, especially the non-REM cycles of sleep. The work of Marcos Frank and Michael Stryker, at University of California–San Francisco, caught the education world by surprise in 2001 with their startling research showing the tremendous amount of branching and subsequent learning that took place during sleep. While most of the science community historically considered that the REM, or dreaming cycle of sleep, was the time when most wiring took place, Stryker's work and the research following that study continue to show that it is actually the non-REM cycles that help hard wire in the information learned the previous day. From a practical standpoint, sleep research continues to show the importance of sleep to the learning brain. Students MUST get sufficient sleep following the learning of new information if we want that information stored in a long-term, complex network of neuron branches" (Kathie F. Nunley, Ed.D., help4teachers.com).

arrive at school bleary-eyed and barely awake. Sports, homework, favorite TV shows, computers, and e-mail often keep preteens up long after they ought to be in bed. Their internal clocks make it easy for them to get their "second wind" just when parents expect them to be as sleepy as they are. No wonder there is often conflict related to going to bed and sleeping. Sleeping well is much more than just a good thing to do—it is a constructive (and necessary) use of time.

❗ *Parenting Tips*

- *Resist allowing your preteen to stay up until midnight on school nights.*

- *Continue to have a consistent bedtime.*

- *Help your child to maintain a bedtime ritual.* Dim lights in the evening and lots of light in the morning can help set the biological clock.

- *Avoid rigorous stimulation from video or computer games late in the evening.* Make evenings as restful as possible.

- *Help your child learn time management strategies to avoid staying up late to do homework.*

- *Make sure your child sleeps in a room without a TV, computer, or cell phone to ensure a calm, quiet atmosphere free of electronic distraction.*

- *Catching up on sleep on weekends (adding an extra hour or two) is fine, but help your preteen avoid oversleeping by many hours, as it confuses the body's natural clock.*

STRESS

Asset 31: Healthy Lifestyle
Asset 32: Planning and Decision Making
Asset 37: Personal Power

Stress is a normal part of life. A healthy amount of stress can actually be beneficial since it helps people keep focused and sharp. When stress becomes unmanageable, problems arise. Managing stress can be especially difficult for preteens, because they do not yet have access to the wisdom of experiences and resources that adults have, including stress-reduction techniques, social contacts, and financial resources.

Bullies, parental discord, sibling rivalry, friendship problems, environmental disasters, school failure, and overcrowded schedules, are all common stressors for preteens. Parents can help minimize stress by setting realistic expectations that reflect an acceptance of children for who they are, not who you want them to be. In this way you can avoid damaging your relationship with your preteens when your dreams for them may differ from their own.

Some kids seem relatively unaffected by everyday stresses, while others are more susceptible to them. Each child is born with a unique temperament. Some are shy, some are outgoing, some are sensitive, and some are boisterous and extroverted. Some move quickly, and others move slowly. How a person handles stress depends upon personality, level of maturity, and coping strategies. Kids who are able to handle stress well also have had good role models who create, maintain, and model a balanced life.

Symptoms of stress in your child can be both physical and behavioral. Stressed preteens can be irritable, tearful, aggressive, or withdrawn. They may experience stomachaches, headaches, or sleeping troubles. Others may develop asthma, hay fever, or migraines, and may cry easily or snap at their siblings. It's important to know that kids may not have the vocabulary or self-awareness to identify their stress and may only be able to identify their symptoms. Tune in to their behavior so that you can help them discover what is causing their distress. Rule out physical illness first and then look for other possible stressors.

❗ *Parenting Tips*

- *Consider how you handle stress.* Do you model a healthy balance between work and home? Examine the eating and sleeping habits you keep, and the ways you resolve conflict with your parenting partner or spouse.

- *Help your preteen find a social group.* Arrange opportunities for your child to socialize. Continue to provide support to your child when it comes to finalizing the details of time, place, and activity.

- *Make sure your child has free time and is not overscheduled with too many activities.* Leave plenty of time for homework, meals, and relaxation, as well as scheduled activities.

- *Encourage "chill time" when nothing is on the calendar and your child can hang out at home, read, do puzzles, paint or draw, and play games.*

- *Teach your child healthy ways to relieve stress:* exercising, napping, deep breathing, journaling, talking to someone, taking a hot bath or shower, sipping a cup of hot cocoa or tea.

- *Help your child learn to identify stress triggers and how to deal with them.*

- *If spiritual practices are a part of your family life, take time to attend services with your faith community where you and your child can gain perspective and recharge your batteries.*

TESTING ISSUES

ASSET 22: Learning Engagement
ASSET 37: Personal Power
ASSET 38: Self-Esteem
ASSET 40: Positive View of Personal Future

The value of giving standardized tests to children has been debated for years. Psychologist Alfred Binet, who pioneered IQ testing in 1904, actually cautioned against misusing the tests, and it was not his intent to suggest that a person's IQ was a fixed state that could not be changed. Modern critics of IQ testing argue that intelligence has not been definitively established and, therefore, cannot be measured. Other critics submit that different tests produce scores that may vary significantly for a single person and are unreliable. The same person may score many points higher or lower, depending upon the test.

Despite Binet's warning, the United States education system maintains the practice of testing students. Critics of standardized testing point out that cultural issues contribute to the unreliability of these tests. Life experiences vary greatly among wealthy, poor, rural, and urban students, and between students of different ethnic cultures. Urban students may perform less well on questions related to farming, and rural students may not fare as well on questions related to mass transit. Such demographic differences influence test scores and may prejudice those who view or interpret the results.

Some schools administer tests to determine whether students are qualified for gifted and talented programs or need special educational services. If students struggle academically or behaviorally, a psychologist tests them to determine why they are not performing as well as their peers. Testing usually begins by determining a child's intelligence quotient (IQ). Many tests are available, including the Wechsler Intelligence Scale for Children (WISC). The results of this test are compared to a child's grades to help determine if there is a discrepancy between ability and performance. If a highly intelligent child is performing poorly in school, there may be further investigation to determine if learning disabilities are present. This test has been used for many years and is considered reliable by those who believe intelligence can be measured.

An intelligence test that is often a better choice for kids with language difficulties is the Comprehensive Test of Nonverbal Intelligence (CTONI). If your child receives a low score on the WISC, and you do not feel it is an accurate assessment of his or her intelligence, ask that the CTONI also be administered.

While IQ test scores are just that—test scores—people tend to believe "objective" data. If a teacher believes a child has ability, he or she treats the child as if there is ability. If children believe they have ability, they will work with the expectation of success. Parents want their children to be perceived as intelligent people who can achieve high expectations with the proper supports. Children who struggle can achieve their goals as long as they have appropriate support. For a list and description of tests that can be used to identify learning issues, see the Dumont Willis Web link at Fairleigh Dickinson University's Web site (alpha.fdu.edu/psychology).

Test scores are personal information. It's important not to share your child's test scores with other people in casual conversation. It is common for people to be curious and to compare their children's test scores with one another to gauge how their child is doing. It is unfair to your child (and to every other child) to share this information, especially given how scores can affect the way people are perceived and treated.

Test scores provide a great opportunity to discuss with your preteen the importance of keeping some information private, and how to make judgments about what should and should not be shared. Kids deserve their privacy. Share testing information only with the teachers, counselors, tutors, and administrators who need the information to adequately serve your child.

You might also consider explaining to your preteen that tests are just "snapshots" in time and are not predictors of what they are capable of achieving. Many successful people have performed poorly on important tests but have done well in real situations. Emotional intelligence, common sense, social skills, charisma, empathy, and humor are often better predictors of life success than the IQ test. To have a positive view of their futures, all children need to view themselves as being full of possibilities. Don't let standardized tests take that away from them or you.

! Parenting Tips

- *Some preteens take tests in stride, viewing them as positive challenges.* Others dread tests so intensely they go blank and are unable to retrieve stored information. If your preteen suffers from test anxiety, try some of the following strategies to make testing manageable.

- *Plan ahead.* Make sure your preteen keeps track of upcoming tests and budgets adequate time for study, review, and sleep.

- *Help preteens recognize physical signs of anxiety so they can learn to manage symptoms before they become severe* (sweaty palms, racing heart, head-ache, stomachache).

- *Teach relaxation techniques when physical symptoms appear:* take deep breaths, visualize, walk around, listen to music, think of something funny, remember positive accomplishments. Positive self-talk is essential.

- *Help preteens view a reasonable amount of anxiety as an ally, rather than an enemy.* Stress can keep you on your toes and enhance performance when it is not overwhelming.

- *Help your preteen come prepared for a test, with paper, pens, pencils, erasers, scrap paper, calculator, and so on.*

- *Make sure your child gets adequate sleep before a test.* Sleep helps solidify information so it can be retrieved when needed.

- *Inform teachers early about your child's anxiety.* Don't wait until the day before a test. Ask for extended testing time for your preteen, if necessary. (Sometimes only students who have been identified as special needs students are entitled by law to extended time on standardized tests.)

WEIGHT AND BODY IMAGE

ASSET 31: Healthy Lifestyle
ASSET 38: Self-Esteem

During the preteen years, bodies are changing as quickly as emotions. If preteens struggle with weight problems, there are sure to be negative impacts on their self-esteem. Unfortunately, obese children often become obese adults with high blood pressure and other physical ailments, such as diabetes, joint problems, and cancer, and are more likely to suffer emotional damage from teasing and ostracism, resulting in a poor self-image.

According to the American Obesity Association, 15.3 percent of U.S. children ages 6 to 11 are obese, with a body mass index of 30 or above. A recent survey by the association reveals that 30 percent of parents are concerned about their child's weight, 12 percent of those parents consider their child to be overweight, and 61 percent said they would change their own eating habits if it meant helping their child maintain a healthy weight (www.obesity.org).

❗ Parenting Tips

- *You are your child's best role model.* Model healthy eating habits and regular exercise. Don't make weight comparisons between your child and other children.

- *If you are concerned about your child's weight, ask your medical doctor about the healthy weight range for your child on his or her growth curve.* Sometimes parents can be overly influenced by the culture's obsession with thinness.

- *Some children put on additional pounds just before puberty and before a growth spurt occurs.* Be concerned only when weight is outside normal ranges for your child's growth curve.

- *Emphasize health rather than weight.* Celebrate milestones or goals that your preteen achieves (for example, walking a mile, climbing the stairs five times, riding a certain distance on a bike).

- *Stock your shelves with healthy snacks like fruit, raw vegetables, nuts, plain popcorn, and low-fat cheese.* Read nutrition labels. Sometimes healthy-sounding snacks like protein bars are loaded with calories. They may be fine for people on the go, but not ideal for people sitting and snacking on a couch.

- *Limit TV watching, video and computer games, and other sedentary activities.* Get up and move as a family. Go for walks, play tennis, or fly a kite. Do anything safe that gets everyone moving and staying physically active. And encourage your preteen to enroll in activities she enjoys, like swimming or baseball. Let her choose.

- *Model eating at a calm pace, and monitor your child's and your own reasonable food portions.* Teach your child to fill up on fresh fruits and vegetables. Limit desserts, other sweets, and carbonated drinks. Encourage him to drink water and low-fat milk.

- *Have everyone participate in household chores that involve movement: vacuuming, mowing the lawn, walking the dog, washing windows.*

- *If you need additional support to help your child create a healthy eating plan, make an appointment with a registered dietitian and nutritionist.* Join your child on the plan, and be mutually supportive (see "Food and Nutrition Information" at the American Dietetic Association's Web site, www.eatright.org).

WORRY AND ANXIETY

Asset 10: Safety
Asset 22: Learning Engagement
Asset 37: Personal Power
Asset 38: Self-Esteem

An appropriate level of concern or worry helps keep us alert and on our toes, but an overabundance of anxiety and fear is unhealthy, both emotionally and physically. Anxiety disorders are the most common mental illnesses in the United States, according to the Mental Health Association of Westchester, New York; about 13 percent of American children and adolescents are affected by anxiety disorders each year (www.mhawestchester.org). Unlike kids who are able to take social and academic stress in stride, anxious preteens may not feel safe or comfortable in regular situations, like school classrooms or parties. To develop assets related to safety, learning engagement, personal power, and self-esteem, it is important for preteens to learn to manage anxiety effectively.

"Anxiety is a subjective sense of worry, apprehension, fear and distress. Anxiety disorders, when severe, can affect a child's thinking, decision-making ability, perceptions of the environment, learning and concentration. Anxiety raises blood pressure and heart rate, and can cause a multitude of bodily complaints, such as nausea, vomiting, stomach pain, ulcers, diarrhea, tingling, weakness, and shortness of breath, among other things. Although quite common, anxiety disorders in children often are overlooked or misjudged, despite being very treatable conditions with good, persistent medical care" (www.keepkidshealthy.com).

ⓘ *Parenting Tips*

- *It's important to determine the root causes of childhood anxiety, so be sure to seek a medical assessment for your preteen if you are concerned.* Anxiety can be confused with symptoms of other common problems (such as AD/HD), and may involve a similar lack of attention and confusion over instructions. An accurate diagnosis is key, because medication for anxiety disorders differs from AD/HD medication.

- *Various anxiety disorders in children and adolescents include separation anxiety disorder, panic disorder, obsessive-compulsive disorder (OCD), post-traumatic stress disorder (PTSD), phobias, and generalized anxiety disorder.* Once properly diagnosed and treated, usually with counseling, medication, relaxation techniques, or in combination, preteens can learn to recognize and deal with their symptoms so that they can feel safe and in control of their lives (www.mhawestchester.org).

EPILOGUE

We started this book humming "Stuck In the Middle with You," but now I hope you are singing a different tune! Armed with new parenting information and the support of other parents, you're better prepared to know what to expect and how to react to issues that may arise during your child's preteen years. If you were to take a long road trip, you would want to have the essentials with you—maps, food, directions, important phone numbers, names of places to visit, spare tire, first aid kit, water, blankets, and money. The preteen parenting journey requires some essentials, too. Probably the most important thing is your positive perspective. A smile, sense of humor, and imagination can turn annoying or difficult situations into learning experiences. And bring along your arms for lots of reassuring hugs!

Demonstrate your values, ethics, and morals so that your preteen can observe you and learn from you. Show him or her the value of building assets—ethical behavior, empathy, respect for others' differences, kindness, and a strong faith. And don't worry if you don't have lots of money to spend. Trust in the notion that your preteen would rather have time with you than lots of material items—even if he or she asks for them! Listen well and really hear what your kids need you to know about them and the world they live in.

The parenting journey is an exciting one. As you travel through your child's preteen years, I wish you joy, happiness, perseverance, and success. Your preteen is lucky to have a parent who is willing to seek out information and strategies that will allow you to be the best parent you can be.

REFERENCES

Ackerman, Mary. *Conversations on the Go: Clever Questions to Keep Teens and Grown Ups Talking,* Minneapolis, MN: Search Institute, 2004.

Benard, Bonnie. *Fostering Resiliency in Kids: Protective Factors in the Home, School, and Community,* Portland, OR: Western Center for Drug Free Schools and Communities, August 1991, 1–27.

Center for Early Adolescence. *Living with 10- to 15-Year-Olds: A Parent Education Curriculum,* Chapel Hill: The University of North Carolina School of Medicine, Center for Early Adolescence, 1992.

Checkley, Kathy. "The First Seven . . . and the Eighth: A Conversation with Howard Gardner," *Educational Leadership* 53:1, 8–13.

Covey, Stephen. *The Seven Habits of Highly Effective People,* New York: Free Press, 1990.

Curwin, Richard L. and Allen N. Mendler. *Discipline with Dignity,* Alexandria, VA: Association for Supervision and Curriculum Development, 1999.

Erikson, Erik H. *Childhood and Society,* New York: W.W. Norton and Co., 1993.

Faber, Adele and Elaine Mazlish. *How to Talk So Kids Will Listen and Listen So Kids Will Talk,* New York: Avon Books, 1999.

Gardner, Howard. *Frames of Mind: The Theory of Multiple Intelligences,* New York: Basic Books, 1983.

Giannetti, Charlene and Margaret Sagarese. *The Rollercoaster Years,* New York: Broadway Books, 1997.

Goleman, Daniel. *Emotional Intelligence: Why It Can Matter More Than IQ,* New York: Bantam, 1995.

Gurian, Michael. *The Wonder of Boys: What Parents, Mentors and Educators Can Do to Shape Boys Into Exceptional Men,* New York: G.P. Putnam's Sons, 1996, 232.

Gurian, Michael and Kathy Stevens. "With Boys and Girls in Mind," *Educational Leadership,* 62:3, 21–26.

Howard, Renie. *When Parents Ask For Help: Everyday Issues Through An Asset-Building Lens,* Minneapolis, MN: Search Institute, 2003.

Mosatche, Harriet S. and Karen Unger. *Too Old For This, Too Young For That: Your Survival Guide For the Middle School Years,* Minneapolis, MN: Free Spirit Publishing, 2000.

Nunley, Kathie F. *How the Adolescent Brain Challenges the Adult Brain,* help4teachers.com/prefrontalcortex.html.

Popham, W. James. *Testing! Testing! What Every Parent Should Know About School Tests,* Boston, MA: Allyn & Bacon, 1999.

Rao, Uma. "Depression and Substance Use Disorders in Adolescents" *The Prevention Researcher* 8:4 (2001), 15–16.

Rosenberg, Ellen. *Get A Clue: What's Really Going On with Preteens and How Parents Can Help,* New York: Owl Books, 1999.

Search Institute, *Developmental Assets: A Profile of Your Youth (Search Institute 2003 Weighted Aggregate Dataset)*, Minneapolis: Search Institute, Report No. 2003, 2005.

Strauch, Barbara. *The Primal Teen: What the New Discoveries About the Teenage Brain Tell Us About Our Kids*, New York: Doubleday, 2003.

Swartz, Karen, M.D. "Recognizing Teenage Depression," *The Prevention Researcher* 8:4, 1–4.

Thomsen, Kate. *Building Resilient Students: Integrating Resiliency Into What You Already Know and Do*, Thousand Oaks, CA.: Corwin Press, 2002.

———— *Service Learning: Experiential Learning That Builds Character and Motivation*, Thousand Oaks, CA.: Corwin Press, 2005.

Walsh, David. *NO: Why Kids of All Ages Need to Hear It and Ways Parents Can Say It*, New York: Free Press, 2007.

Walsh, David and Nat Bennett. *WHY Do They Act That Way? A Survival Guide to the Adolescent Brain for You and Your Teen*, New York: Free Press, 2004.

Wiseman, Rosalind. *Queen Bees and Wannabes: Helping Your Daughter Survive Cliques, Gossip, Boyfriends, and Other Realities of Adolescence*, New York: Crown Publishers, 2002.

Wolfe, Patricia. *Brain Matters: Translating Research into Classroom Practice*, Alexandria, VA: Association for Supervision and Curriculum Development, 2001.

ONLINE RESOURCES

In addition to print references listed in References, you'll find helpful information and support on various topics at the following Web sites:

After-School Time and Latchkey Hours
- After-School All-Stars: www.afterschoolallstars.org
- Arlington (VA) Police Department: www.arlingtonva.us
- Kids Help Line (Australia): www.kidshelp.com.au
- MSN Encarta: encarta.msn.com

Alcohol, Tobacco, and Other Drugs
- The Alberta (Canada) Alcohol and Drug Abuse Commission: www.aadac.com
- National Center on Addiction and Substance Abuse (Columbia University): www.casacolumbia.org
- National Institute on Drug Abuse: www.nida.nih.gov
- Nemours Foundation/KidsHealth: www.kidshealth.org
- University of Michigan Monitoring the Future Study: www.monitoringthefuture.org

Anger Management and Conflict Resolution
- North Carolina State University Family and Consumer Sciences: www.ces.ncsu.edu/depts/fcs
- North Dakota State University Extension Service: www.ext.nodak.edu
- PBS Kids/Emotions: pbskids.org/itsmylife
- The Positive Way: www.positive-way.com

Anxiety and Worry
- American Academy of Child and Adolescent Psychiatry: www.aacap.org
- Keep Kids Healthy (Vincent Iannelli, M.D.): www.keepkidshealthy.com

- Mental Health Association of Westchester County (NY): www.mhawestchester.org
- Nemours Foundation/KidsHealth: www.kidshealth.org

Attention Disorders (AD/HD)
- Children and Adults with Attention Deficit/ Hyperactivity Disorder: www.chadd.org
- Keep Kids Healthy (Vincent Iannelli, M.D.): www.keepkidshealthy.com
- Medline Plus (National Library of Medicine/National Institutes of Health): www.nlm.nih.gov/medlineplus

Auditory Processing Disorder
- American Speech-Language-Hearing Association: www.asha.org
- National Coalition on Auditory Processing Disorders: www.ncapd.org
- National Institute on Deafness and Other Communication Disorders: www.nidcd.nih.gov
- Nemours Foundation/KidsHealth: www.kidshealth.org

Brain Development
- National Institute for Mental Health: www.nimh.nih.gov
- Neuroscience for Kids: faculty.washington.edu/chudler/dev.html
- NIH Neuroscientist Jay Geidd, M.D. (PBS Frontline): www.pbs.org
- Society for Neuroscience (About Neuroscience links): www.sfn.org

Bullying
- BullyStoppers: www.bullystoppers.com
- Committee for Children: www.cfchildren.org
- Olweus Bullying Prevention Program (Clemson University): www.clemson.edu/olweus
- Pennsylvania State University Extension Service: resiliency.cas.psu.edu
- Promoting Relationships and Preventing Violence Network (PREVNet): www.prevnet.ca

- U.S. Health Resources and Services Administration: www.stopbullyingnow.hrsa.gov
- Wired Safety/Parry Aftab, J.D.: www.stopcyberbullying.org

Caring and Safe Homes
- Center for Social and Emotional Education: www.csee.net
- PBS "The New Heroes": www.pbs.org

Choking Game
- Connect with Kids: www.connectwithkids.com
- The Dylan Blake Foundation: www.chokinggameinformation.com
- G.A.S.P.: www.stop-the-choking-game.com

Community Service and Contributing to the Common Good
- Learn and Serve America: www.learnandserve.org
- National Service-Learning Clearinghouse: www.servicelearning.org
- National Youth Leadership Council: www.nylc.org

Crushes and Dating
- Children, Youth and Families Education and Research Network: cyfernet.ces.ncsu.edu
- iParenting: preteenagerstoday.com
- KidsHealth: www.kidshealth.org
- Parenting Adolescents: parentingteens.about.com
- TeenLink/University of Minnesota Extension Service: www.teenlink.umn.edu

Depression (Childhood and Preteen)
- Healthy Place.com: www.healthyplace.com/communities/depression/children_6.asp
- National Alliance on Mental Illness: www.nami.org
- Palo Alto Medical Foundation: www.pamf.org/preteen
- Wing of Madness: www.wingofmadness.com/articles/children.htm

Divorce, Separation, and Single Parenting
- American Academy of Child and Adolescent Psychiatry: www.aacap.org
- Children First/University of Minnesota Extension Service: www.parenting.umn.edu
- Kids First Center: www.kidsfirstcenter.org
- Single Parents: singleparents.about.com

Eating Disorders
- Family Doctor/American Academy of Family Physicians: familydoctor.org
- Mirasol Eating Disorder Recovery: www.mirasol.net
- National Association of Anorexia Nervosa and Associated Disorders: www.anad.org
- National Eating Disorders Association: www.nationaleatingdisorders.org
- National Women's Health Information Center: www.4woman.gov

Gambling
- Alberta (Canada) Drug and Alcohol Abuse Commission: www.aadac.com
- Illinois Institute for Addiction Recovery: www.addictionrecov.org
- McGill University International Center for Youth Gambling: www.youthgambling.com
- YMCA Youth Gambling Program: www.ymcatoronto.org

Grief
- American Academy of Child and Adolescent Psychiatry: aacap.org
- Children's Grief and Loss: www.childrensgrief.net
- Tufts University Child and Family WebGuide: www.cfw.tufts.edu

Human Development
- American Academy of Pediatrics: www.aap.org
- The Gesell Institute of Human Development: www.gesellinstitute.org

- The Media Project:
  www.themediaproject.com/facts/development/9_12.htm
- The Parent Report.com: www.theparentreport.com
- Schwab Learning: www.schwablearning.org

Internet Use and Safety
- America Online Acronyms: www.aim.com
- FBI Parent's Guide to Internet Safety: www.fbi.gov
- Safe Kids—Guidelines for Parents and Kids:
  safekids.com/family-contract-for-online-safety
- Wired Safety: www.wiredsafety.org

Learning Disabilities
- KidSource Online:
  www.kidsource.com/NICHCY/learning_disabilities.html
- National Center for Learning Disabilities:
  www.ncld.org
- National Dissemination Center for Children with
  Disabilities: www.nichcy.org
- PBS Parents:
  www.pbs.org/parents/strugglingtolearn/resources.htm

Learning Styles and Multiple Intelligences
- Howard Gardner, Ph.D.: www.howardgardner.com
- Leslie Wilson, Ed.D.: www.uwsp.edu/Education/
  lwilson/learning/miindicators.htm
- Thomas Armstrong, Ph.D.:
  www.thomasarmstrong.com/multiple_intelligences.htm
- Portland State University Department of Psychology:
  www.psy.pdx.edu/PsiCafe

Obesity in Childhood
- American Heart Association: www.americanheart.org
- Children's Nutrition Research Center (Baylor College of
  Medicine): www.kidsnutrition.org
- KidSource Online: www.kidsource.com
- The Obesity Society: www.obesity.org

Precocious Puberty

- American Academy of Pediatrics: www.aap.org
- Nemours Foundation/Kids Health: www.kidshealth.org
- Pediatrics—About.com: pediatrics.about.com/cs/conditions/a/early_puberty.htm
- Women's Healthcare: www.womenshealthcaretopics.com/teen_sexuality.htm

Sexual Identity

- Advocates for Youth: www.advocatesforyouth.org
- Parents, Families and Friends of Lesbians and Gays: www.pflag.org
- University of Texas/Dallas: www.utdallas.edu/counseling/selfhelp

Sleep Needs

- American Academy of Family Physicians/Family Doctor: www.kidshealth.org
- McGill University Health Centre: www.muhc.ca/media/ensemble/2005jan/pre_teen_sleep
- Parent Report: www.theparentreport.com
- PBS Frontline: www.pbs.org

Stress

- Nemours Foundation/KidsHealth: www.kidshealth.org
- New York University Child Study Center: www.aboutourkids.org
- Robyn's Nest—The Parenting Network: www.robynsnest.com

Testing Issues

- Dumont Willis/Fairleigh Dickinson University: alpha.fdu.edu/psychology
- Family Education Network: school.familyeducation.com
- KidSource Online Parents: www.kidsource.com
- National Center for Fair and Open Testing: www.fairtest.org

INDEX

ABOUT THE AUTHOR

Kate Thomsen, M.A., C.A.S., is a New York-based author, speaker, and education consultant. She is the author of *Building Resilient Students: Integrating Resiliency into Everything You Already Know and Do* and *Service-Learning in Grades K–8*, both published by Corwin Press. Ms. Thomsen previously worked for the Onondaga-Cortland-Madison Board of Cooperative Educational Services in Syracuse, N.Y., where she provided staff development for schools on topics ranging from emotional literacy to positive youth development to a variety of high-risk issues. Ms. Thomsen is a co-founder of Prevention Partners for Youth Development and a former adjunct professor at Syracuse University. She has two grown sons and lives with her husband in Jamesville, New York. She can be reached at kftconsult@twcny.rr.com.

REVIEWER ACKNOWLEDGMENTS

Search Institute extends sincere thanks to the following individuals who reviewed an early draft of the manuscript and added their professional insights: Mary Ackerman, Sherry Boyce, Kate Brielmaier, Scott Butler, Alison Dotson, Nancy Grant, Bonnie Granatir, Debbie Grillo, Pat Howell-Blackmore, Linda Rhubright, Patsy Roybal, Carmen Stephens, and Terri Swanson.

ABOUT SEARCH INSTITUTE PRESS

Search Institute Press is a division of Search Institute, a nonprofit organization that offers leadership, knowledge, and resources to promote positive youth development. Our mission at Search Institute Press is to provide practical and hope-filled resources to help create a world in which all young people thrive. Our products are embedded in research, and the 40 Developmental Assets®—qualities, experiences, and relationships youth need to succeed—are a central focus of our resources. Our logo, the SIP flower, is a symbol of the thriving and healthy growth young people experience when they have an abundance of assets in their lives.